THE VISION AND IMPACT OF FETHULLAH GÜLEN

A NEW PARADIGM FOR SOCIAL ACTIVISM

THE VISION AND IMPACT OF FETHULLAH GÜLEN

A NEW PARADIGM FOR SOCIAL ACTIVISM

Maimul Ahsan Khan

BLUE DOME

Published by Bluedome Press
535 Fifth Avenue, 6th Fl
New York, NY 10017

www.bluedomepress.com

Library of Congress Cataloging-in-Publication Data Available

ISBN: 978-1-935295-09-9

Printed by
Çağlayan A.Ş., Izmir - Turkey

CONTENTS

INTRODUCTION

Fethullah Gülen has been a household name in modern Turkey for several decades now. In 2008, he was recognized as the most influential intellectual in the world in a global public poll jointly conducted by *Foreign Policy*, the American award-winning magazine of global politics, and Britain's *Prospect* magazine. Trained in the religious sciences by several celebrated Muslim scholars and spiritual masters in Eastern Turkey, Gülen has also studied the principles and theories of modern social and physical sciences. In 1959, after receiving excellent examination results, he started his professional career as an Islamic preacher endorsed by the government authorities in Ankara. Though he had to follow all instructions given directly and indirectly by the ultra-secular government for his preaching to be tolerated by those who held political and military power at the time, in the course of performing his official and unofficial duties as a Muslim cleric, preacher, and social activist, he managed to develop a rigorous religious and intellectual discourse. While keeping his distance from all controversy in the political affairs of the country, Gülen has continuously asked his compatriots to do what they need to do for positive reform and for the welfare of the people and the world in general and for the improvement of Turkey's performance on the world stage. His innovative ideas about educational and social reforms have already proven invaluable to society in general and Muslim communities in particular.

Unlike many other Muslim preachers and authors, Gülen has never confined himself to a narrow arena of traditional or national religious thinking. He has not blamed particular governments for all the miseries his own people and that of others. He has spoken out on behalf of the oppressed and ignored masses for and with whom he has been looking for new paradigms of religious discourse and activism. However, instead of focusing on specific social, economic, or political viewpoints, his call for reforms has been on behalf of and directed at all segments of the population, including the political and business elite. Avoiding all kinds of confrontational strategies and partisan politics, Gülen has relentlessly continued his call for unity and harmony among all people based on the peaceful teachings of Islam. Clearly, and in theoretical terms, this is nothing new in the Islamic tradition of Sufi movements or Sufism. In the past, there were many Sufi movements very close to the ideals that have been preached by Gülen. However, Gülen is neither a mystic nor a Sufi in any traditional sense.

Gülen and those inspired by him have presented a new kind of Islamic intellectualism and altruism coupled with a deeper sense of activism and spirituality that has been missing from many contemporary Muslim movements. The failure of many politically-based Muslim movements around the world finds no reflection in the preaching and writing style of Gülen. The revival of other religious groups or non-Islamic religious traditions has not discouraged Gülen in any way from shaping his own ideals of spreading value-based education and people-oriented spirituality and cultural activities.

Since the late decades of the twentieth century, humankind has been turning in large numbers to religious and spiritual ideals for protection and growth as the human race that is deemed to be the supreme creature on earth. With respect to this renewed seeking, Gülen argues that since many genuine Islamic religious ideals have been either lost or distorted, the turning of numerous religious groups and parties to religious doctrines has led to the creation and establishment of fanatical or ultra-orthodox forces in politics. The situation in the Western world is not different. Indeed, the history of modern Christian fundamentalism also goes back to the early decades of the twentieth century.

With the emergence of Muslim nation states on the political map of the world, different kinds of extreme religious indoctrination have harmed the genuine revival of universal Islamic values. Gülen's preaching and writing demonstrate that he is quite aware of this intellectual inability of the political movements of his many predecessors to uphold the moral and ethical values derived from the Qur'an and Islamic traditions. A good number of Muslim countries have attempted to prosper while basing themselves on nationalist ideals. Like many Arabs and Persians, in the early years of the Republic many Turks also seemed to want to build a prosperous modern state based solely on nationalist ideals and thus tended to show a discriminatory attitude toward all kinds of religious traditions and phenomena based on religious beliefs.

Many Islamic religious symbols were either misused or attacked disproportionately in the political games of capturing and upholding state power. Gülen's voice of moderation surfaced at this juncture of a dichotomous Muslim polity and the ideological struggles between extreme forces in the Muslim world. Gülen preached the path of moderation, honesty, and sincerity to protect the interests of the masses, irrespective of the ethnicity or the religious practice of particular groups of people.

Unlike some religious leaders and clerics in other parts of the world who are his contemporaries, Gülen has never aimed to overthrow a secular government and replace it with a religiously based political party. He has never considered this as an option to eliminate corruption within the state and political system. Gülen finds this unacceptable as it contradicts the core principle of the noncompulsory character of Islamic religious practice and no state or society can be truly transformed merely by such partisan politics. Thus, Gülen has always been very careful in his preaching and writings to balance his call for sound education with universal values to build a virtuous society.

Many analysts and authors have called Gülen the modern-day Rumi of Turkey, the land where Rumi was put to rest for eternity in the city of Konya. Rumi, the renowned thirteenth-century poet, philosopher, and mystic, is celebrated by both Turks and Iranians, but he is also a matter of contestation between the two nations regarding his ethnic identity. However, Rumi's Sufi traditions cut across the lines between nationalistic and sectarian differences, and the truth of the matter is that eight hundred years ago, national and ethnic identity played a very insignificant role in determining someone's contribution to Muslim civilization. In practice, Gülen has brought that glorious tradition back to the minds of millions of modern and religious Turks.

Gülen is neither a poet nor a mystic in its traditional or typical sense, but perhaps his series of writings on Sufism has earned him the title of Sufi. Gülen's preaching is full of compassion for all, and none of his writings ignite any kind of hatred against anyone. That might be one of the reasons why Gülen has been considered seriously as a Sufi. A second reason could be his lifelong personal piety and austere lifestyle.

While Muslims would probably not call Gülen a Mahatma Gandhi of Turkey or the Muslim world, some Westerners have started to call him a Muslim Gandhi.[1] In the substance of his preaching and writing, Gülen is a voice very close to both Rumi and Gandhi; he has always sought truth in bringing people together for the causes of peace and humanity for all, irrespective of race and religion. Like Rumi, Gandhi also never abandoned any of his own religious traditions. However, both of them were disliked, even hated, by many of their orthodox co-worshipers for their extraordinary humility towards the followers of other religions. Gandhi was killed in 1948 by a Hindu fundamentalist who, like many other orthodox Hindus, believed that Gandhi was betraying the cause of the Hindu religion and that he was influenced by the Muslim intellectuals of British India and the Sufis of South Africa. Away from the persecution of false accusations of igniting religious hatred in Turkey, Gülen lives in the USA where he has proven himself a champion of the cause of interfaith dialogue and bringing people of all races and religions together to work for peace and harmony between nations and religions.

Many Muslim authors seem to believe that the modern Western mind is too materialistic to favor the core universal spiritual message of Islam. Thus, many Muslim analysts tend to conclude that it is useless to preach Islamic values to Westerners. Gülen does not accept this simplistic presentation of Western materialism as a barrier to spreading the peaceful message of the Qur'an and Sunnah upon which a compassionate society can be built. He does not believe that Westerners have any inherent problem in appreciating and accepting the spirituality derived from the fundamental sources of Islam; for him the question is how well Muslims can represent Islamic spirituality and the universal message of Islam so as to attract Westerners to build a global society based on genuine equality, tranquility, and humane treatment for all, irrespective of gender, race, and religion.

Gülen advocates a compassionate and brotherly form of Islam that emphasizes inner spirituality rather than an aggressive, outer expression of religious beliefs and coercive propaganda. In rediscovering this fine line of spirituality, Gülen has skillfully avoided the tendency to overemphasize a particular set of characteristics that might be seen as belonging to western or eastern, northern or southern people. He is critical of any kind of nationalistic or ethnic confrontational policies which lead to discriminatory attitudes to others, or dividing people between "us" and "them."

His definition of nation does not compromise one race or ethnic group; Anatolia has always been a land of diverse ethnic groups and forms one united nation today. Free of any chauvinism, he addresses the colorful mosaic of Anatolia as "a crucible for peoples that have come from Central Asia, the Balkans, and Mesopotamia."[2] Extrapolation of this notion automatically leads to the principle that the whole of humankind is the offspring of Adam and Eve. Gülen insists on seeing the potential for good in all peoples and religions. He stresses the merit of good deeds and rejects the empty words of hostile propaganda and ways of terrorizing others.

Gülen believes that all human beings have an urge and need to achieve spiritual salvation expressed in their ability to appreciate the heavenly attributes which surround everybody in this world up to the end of physical existence on this planet. Gülen sees the world and human existence on earth as an open book of God Almighty, and the Qur'an is the glorious reflection of the process of the revelation of truth to the whole of humankind. Reading such thoughts in Gülen's books or hearing them from him directly, many observers have believed that he is ultimately a Sufi cleric and therefore his messages will not attract the younger generation of Muslims in secular Turkey and elsewhere, whom they assume to be hot-blooded and radical. This assumption has found no ground in reality, however, as most of those inspired by him are young people.

Gülen is very active religiously and socially while apparently very reluctant to play any part in the political moves of particular political parties or forces. As a non-political entity, Gülen has become something of a center of gravity for many millions of Turkish people from all walks of life. Thus, even secular political parties have tried to use his style of preaching and argumentation to reach out to the voters. However, in his own life he is quite secluded from all kinds of political activities.

Some Westerners view Gülen's way of life as monastic in the Eastern style. They may even see him as a Muslim Dalai Lama seeking *nirvana* throughout his entire life. However, even in his self-imposed exile in the USA, he has never aspired to any media attention or publicity or popularity of any kind. He is deeply involved in interfaith activities and devoted to his Islamic duties as a true Muslim sacrificing every moment and everything quietly for the benefit of others.

In his preaching and writing, Gülen does not devote much time to explaining the differences between Shi'as and Sunnis, Hanafis and Hanbalis, Malikis and Shafi'is, whereas many contemporary Muslim scholars give the utmost importance to these differences of *madhhabs*, or Islamic schools of thought. According to such scholars, focusing on these distinctions is the right way to purify the Muslim community from *shirk* (any belief contrary to the oneness of God) and *bid'a* (any illegitimate innovation in religious affairs), as well as deviation from the *sirat'ul-mustaqim*, or the straight path demonstrated by the Prophet of Islam.

For Gülen, however, the most important thing is to establish a close relation between the human self and the Attributes of God Almighty. Besides, we can hope to regain the lost glory of the Muslim civilization and the generosity and liberality of the Muslim community only when a great number of people are selflessly and honestly devoted to the higher spiritual cause prescribed by the holy ideals of Islam in making the entire human race preserve and protect its own dignity and surroundings for the benefit of all. Gülen does not believe that much can be achieved for these noble causes through military or political means. Dialogue and diplomacy are better options for all sides in any ongoing conflict. Welfare-oriented governance is the best alternative to the corporate greed for profit and deception of all kinds aimed at making money for a tiny group of people in society.

Unlike most Muslim nations, Turks have never experienced direct foreign colonial rule of any kind. This unique feature of the Turkish nation has made them more readily able to reflect upon the universality of Islam, making it possible for them to peacefully co-exist and develop the kind of dialogue that has been expressed or reflected in thousands of Gülen's sermons and in the numerous speeches delivered to Muslim congregations and interfaith meetings both in Turkey and the USA. Those ideas are crystallized in dozens of books written by Gülen. Alongside his preaching about universal values, Gülen has always been mindful of the troubles afflicting the hearts and minds of Turkish people. Knowing very well the risks of alienating himself from some of his own people, he has nevertheless shown great enthusiasm for reform of the education system in

Turkey. In doing this, however, he has never allowed any sect, group, or political party to own or disown him completely. His strategy is very clear: whoever does good and honest work as a Muslim, I should be with him, and I must avoid all kinds of bad or wicked works.

Ultra-secularist forces have tried unsuccessfully to use Gülen for their own political ends in various ways. One attempt was to characterize him as an innovator of religious reforms with little compatibility with the preaching and life of the Prophet Muhammad, peace and blessings be upon him. Having failed in that, some anti-Islamic forces inside and outside Turkey are now trying to portray Gülen as the future Khomeini of Turkey. But Khomeini's year-long stay in the city of Bursa in Turkey, once the capital of the Ottoman Empire, and his exposure to the Sunni communities in Turkey and Iraq did not make him Sunni, and Gülen's exposure to the USA will not make him a revolutionary or worldly Islamic preacher. Gülen's beardless face and modern dress do not make him less Islamic, but he is neither a fanatic nor a so-called modernist incapable of appreciating the Attributes of God Almighty. Comparing Gülen's educational and cultural movement with Khomeini's revolution in Iran is either a reflection of ignorance about the many diverse methods of social reform with wide-ranging ramifications for the revival of Islamic values, or shows a complete lack of knowledge about the many dissimilarities between these two great Muslim nations.

Gülen has always strived for the promotion of good and prevention of evil in his writings, sermons, and speeches. He has opted for positive action and an active form of spiritual *jihad* to transform people by the pen and the tongue, bringing about a revolution in their minds to reach spiritual perfection and to help others do so. His call for spiritual *jihad* with his Sufi-oriented message of love and compassion has nothing to do with war, violence, or even aggressive ways of spreading religious messages.

Our interest in our environment and our love for humankind—that is, our ability to embrace creation—depends on knowing and understanding our own essence, our ability to discover ourselves, and to feel a connection with our Creator...Humanism is a doctrine of love and humanity which is articulated recklessly these days, and it has a potential to be easily manipulated through different interpretations. Some circles try to impose an abstract and unbalanced understanding of humanism by confusing people about *jihad* in Islam and awakening suspicion in their hearts...*Jihad* can be a matter of self-defense or of removing obstacles between God and human free choice.[3]

For many years now, Western commentators have asked why world-renowned Muslim and non-Muslim authors fail to demonstrate any clarity in the complicated issues related to Islam and *jihad*. In this area, Gülen is a voice of complete clarity and consistency in his presentation of Islamic issues and their correlation with universal humanitarianism. Thus, Gülen has filled, at least to some extent, an intellectual gap between the Muslim world and the West.

In turn, questioning or challenging the universality of Western concepts of human rights is rather an easy job. However, empty talk about human rights and humanism does not bring any positive change to the welfare of any nation or humankind. Here, unlike the founders of many Muslim political parties and movements engaged in preaching Islamic values around the world, Gülen does not present any particular Muslim nation state as a suitable model for a comprehensive system of Islamic governance.

Instead, the Gülen movement has initiated the gigantic task of presenting a comprehensive and better alternative to a Western consumption-based society in the areas of educational and cultural exchange between religions and nations.

Even Gülen himself may not be able to imagine the impact he is having now on the Turkish public psyche and beyond in formulating a new and completely peaceful strategy to bridge the East and West or the Muslim world and the rest of the world. This is truly a huge intellectual advance wrought almost single-handedly by Gülen and based on his convincing arguments for peace and dignity for the whole of humankind. His emphasis on a value-based educational system without indoctrination is shown clearly in all his books. This emphasis has led to the founding of hundreds of schools all around the world sponsored by Turkish educators and businessmen where teachers are trying to implement sublime ideals in a value-based educational system.

There is still more to say about the Turkish and Sunni features of the Gülen movement as it has been spearheaded by Sunni Muslims of Turkish origin. One might inquire into how an ultra-secular state such as Turkey could have produced a social, cultural, and educational reformer like Gülen. However, it seems life-long dedication to the universal causes of Islam and humanity may ultimately produce such a result. People inspired by Gülen never indulge in nationalistic, sectarian, or chauvinistic agendas in propagating Islamic values or an educational and cultural system within Muslim communities and beyond. This is the key to the remarkable success of the Gülen movement today. That is what has made him a living legend and, of course, the world's most influential intellectual of 2008.

OUTLINE OF THE BOOK

At the time of writing this book on Gülen's contribution to the spiritual, religious and political thought of Islam and civilizational issues, Gülen emerged as the number one public intellectual of the world in a poll jointly conducted by *Foreign Policy* and *Prospect* magazines in 2008. Many contemporary Muslim intellectuals and religious leaders have written many books to explain the basic tenets of Islam and how to approach and use them in the context of modernity and a technologically driven industrialized society and state. So, Gülen's topic does not seem to be new. However, throughout his life as an author and preacher since the early 1960s, Gülen has formulated his ideas in such a way that an intelligent mind has to give them serious thought before accepting or rejecting any of his descriptions of Islamic values, humanity, and interfaith activities.

As an exponent of Islamic ideals and values, Gülen takes into consideration all kinds of diversity within the different *madhhab*s, or Islamic schools of thought and *tariqa*s, or Sufi religious orders, and does not favor any of the major schools of thought in a way that would undermine the others. Gülen has sought new ways of contemplating and approaching Sufism, religious practice, and spirituality. He has successfully conveyed a comprehensive vision that can easily encompass many complex and controversial issues in both "political" and "spiritual" Islam, a vision that would not easily provoke any sitting secular or even anti-Islamic regime. Gülen's compassionate attitude toward all human beings irrespective of religious faith and political belief has brought him to the center of Islamic spirituality that has been undermined and misinterpreted in the writings of many of his contemporaries in Muslim countries around the world.

The political constraints Gülen has faced in his homeland at times appeared to be an intolerable burden for his spiritual and intellectual development. Facing such obstacles in the painful journey of enlightenment of his own people, Bediüzzaman Said Nursi (1877–1960), the author of the *Risale-i Nur* collection and a most effective and profound representative of Islam's intellectual, moral, and spiritual strengths, once told his brothers and sisters in faith that he always sought refuge in God from Satan and politics. In the writings of Gülen, one can easily observe that he has never tried to convey overly political or doctrinaire messages and often shows respect for Nursi's strategy for the reformation of Turkish society in accordance with the level of its maturity in political thinking and spirituality. In analyzing Gülen's thought as expressed in his books, I humbly try to show that Gülen has expanded on Nursi's ideas in many ways and added more visible dimensions with new heights to that religio-cultural movement based on spiritual activism with ever-expanding horizons of intellectual development.

Gülen has been accepted as a modern Rumi in various religious and nationalist circles in Turkey as he could not be considered an orthodox cleric. In a state like Turkey with a small but powerful and militant secularist elite, it was indeed difficult to subscribe openly to many orthodox religious ideas in preaching Islamic values. In spite of his moderation, some militant secularists try to portray Gülen as a fundamentalist preacher to discredit him as a preacher of Islamic values that have immense potential to reform any society in a better direction. Rumi was a mystic and poet first, and a minimalist in spreading and preaching Islam. Rumi's era also did not allow him to become an active preacher in the first place, whereas Gülen's situation has been improved by the spiritual legacy of Bediüzzaman ("the Wonder of the Age") Said Nursi.

> Bediüzzaman saw this [twentieth] century and its events and the rise of materialism and communism in the context of the end of time and insisted above all else that what took precedence in the struggle against these was the saving and strengthening of belief. It is also in this context that Bediüzzaman's insistence on the way of 'positive action' and 'peaceful *jihad*' or '*jihad* of the word' (*manawi jihad*) for the Risale-i Nur students should be seen. ....As time passes, Bediüzzaman's statements and predictions concerning the future become realized, his judgments as to which course of action should be taken are proved correct, and his greatness and importance become clearer. At a time when the Islamic world was apparently crushed beneath the heel of Europe, he foretold its rise and saw the Qur'an holding sway over the future, the age of science and reason.[4]

Gülen has echoed the voices of Rumi and Nursi in his own way to encourage more people worldwide to join the peaceful march of the Turkish common people, who have experienced many undue constraints and pressure because of their natural inclination toward Islamic values and Muslim culture. The first chapter of this book focuses on this vital issue of conflict between politically based

Islamic ideologies and predominantly spiritual and cultural Islam. This chapter attempts to show that Gülen has always tried to balance the exercise of Islamic spirituality and social activism so as to bring Muslims in particular and people in general to make self sacrifices for the welfare of the complete cross section of society.

The second chapter continues the theme of the first chapter, but here I examine Gülen's understanding of "Sufism in Theory and Practice" in his *Emerald Hills of the Heart: Key Concepts in the Practice of Sufism* series. For Gülen, Sufism is not hollow ideological or religious thinking. Nor is it merely a self-indulgent mystic or hermetic way of thinking and living, but rather it is a comprehensive search and continuous quest for eternal happiness through obedience to God's will. Islam is a comprehensive system designed to bring good and avoid evil in every aspect of life from cradle to death. A Muslim may say that there is nothing new in this assumption or thesis. However, in the face of the severe onslaught of militant secularism, nationalism, materialism, and consumerism against religious values in the current era, this Islamic thesis needed to be recast to make it applicable to the educational and social system of society. The focal point of the second chapter, therefore, is an appreciation of the many connecting channels to Islamic spirituality through religious ritual and social activism which are indicated by Gülen in his books. I have attempted to show how Gülen demystifies many complicated concepts and exercises of the Sufi way of life and accommodates them within the broader boundary of Islamic law; that is, he offers us permissible ways of creativity within the parameters of Islamic legal and moral understanding.

In the third chapter, "Gülen's Methodology of Schooling: Educational Enlightenment at Home and Abroad," I consider the achievements of the educational system inspired by Gülen, who, on the one hand, has advocated value-based education while on the other hand, he warned his ardent supporters not to indulge in politicized or overly doctrinaire teaching styles. The core idea is for the educator to be the living embodiment of universal Islamic values, setting a good example and modeling universal Islamic values without imposing them on any person or community. After the collapse of the Soviet Union and the communist regimes in Eastern European countries, many nations have started to wonder how a value-based educational system might emerge again to replace the previous compulsory, socialist-style, anti-religious school system.

So far in the name of Islamic education, we have mostly witnessed a distorted relationship between the obligatory rituals prescribed by the tenets of Islam and the objectives those rituals are intended to achieve. Mere outward observation of faith in daily, weekly, monthly, and yearly rituals may mask the real state of affairs of a Muslim nation and society. Nationalist and secularist Turkey did not have this problem, but the religious sectors of society needed to be aware that using rituals to camouflage or demonstrate one's identity is a dangerous practice leading to utter hypocrisy which must be avoided at all times.

Gülen dedicated himself to developing a better and humane education for all without seeking publicity for his religious works. Gülen has practiced his spiritual and religious values in complete self sacrifice without asking for any tangible or intangible return from any quarter benefited by his mission. Gülen asks people not to stint in any way in establishing schools that will serve as models for others. His call is aimed at those who are willing to dedicate their entire life to providing better education for children of all races and religions and for people and children without any religious beliefs or practice. How to demonstrate moderation and decency in manners and etiquette with excellent professional standards and achievements is one of the main concerns of Gülen's teaching, which we discuss in this chapter.

In chapter four, "Gülen's Approach to the Qur'an and the Ideal Society," we discuss how Qur'anic teachings are essential and beneficial to build a solid foundation for an ideal social system where human dignity can be preserved and protected for all irrespective of creed and culture. To all Muslim communities and scholars, the

Qur'an is the center of gravity of all Islamic political, legal, economic, and cultural thought. However, misunderstanding about the Qur'anic message is rampant in every Muslim nation and community. Gülen has been very cautious in explaining and referring to Qur'anic verses as the Qur'an is the only divinely ordained source of intellectual and spiritual development for all human beings. Gülen has taken the Qur'anic message as the culmination of all divine revelations and the entire chain of all prophetic wisdom and traditions to pursue the ultimate task of establishing justice on earth for all. No good objective can be achieved through *dhulm* (injustice, cruelty, and exploitation) in any society. Injustice is the real evil for all societies. This Qur'anic message has been brought into light afresh by Gülen's writing in the context of modernity and the technological world in many different ways, and this is the main theme of our discussion in this chapter.

There exists a serious misconception that no nation or state can build or run a functional and prosperous system with the Qur'anic message. Unfortunately, the poor condition of most Muslim nation states contributes a lot to this false assumption as most Muslim nation states have failed to live up to an adequate standard of creativity, productivity, and nurturance of human values for everybody. Arising from the Muslim world, the activities of the Gülen movement throughout the world are significant in this regard. Gülen's concern for the whole of humankind and global civilization is highlighted in chapter five, "Gülen's Notion of *Hizmet* and the Public Good: From a Strategy to an Action Plan." One can clearly see that Gülen is not a simple theoretician or philosopher who is reluctant to deal with hard questions of reality. He offers his ideas to his audience to make them aware and responsible so that they may create a golden generation who will be dedicated to building a just society for all. Alongside the preceding chapter, this chapter may be regarded as the soul of the book's main theme, which is how to build a better human society that can be appreciated and enjoyed by every human being.

In the following chapter, "Gülen's Thoughts on Modern Democracy," I try to explain that Gülen's writings are very much in line with democratic thought. However, for Gülen substantially Islamic values are helpful for the emergence of a genuinely democratic system and good governance. In almost every society today the issue of the public good is often ignored or confused with material gain only, whereas Gülen has argued very strongly that without spiritual awakening, neither an individual nor a society can achieve true prosperity and emancipation. Gülen's main proposition is that Islam does not prescribe any particular form or method of governance for any state or society for all time. From his own words, we can recognize that Gülen is very clear in his views about the relationship between a system of governance and the teachings of Islam.

> Islam as a religion focuses primarily on the immutable aspects of life and existence, whereas a political system concerns only social aspects of our worldly life. Islam's basic principles of belief, worship, morality, and behavior are not affected by changing times. Islam does not propose a certain unchangeable form of government or attempt to shape it. Islam has never offered nor established a theocracy in its name. Instead, Islam establishes fundamental principles that orient a government's general character. So, politics can be a factor neither in shaping Islam nor directing Muslims' acts and attitudes in Islam's name.[5]

Once one understands this major thesis, which Gülen has explained in his many writings, speeches, and interviews, it becomes easier for the researcher or reader to appreciate how Muslims can coexist peacefully with the followers of other religions. Islam respects any peaceful attempt of a true believer in God Almighty to bring people of different religions and ideologies together to achieve common objectives of peace and tranquility in the personal and public life of all people. The Gülen movement, as many observers now call it, has been doing this for more than four decades in Turkey and beyond.

The last chapter, "Gülen on *Jihad*, Tolerance and Terrorism," is a kind of conclusion to the book. This chapter demonstrates how deeply the movement is concerned with achieving at least some basic common goals for the whole of humanity. Here Gülen's interpretations of the Qur'anic message or the universal message of Islam are compatible with modern universal human rights. The Gülen movement does not accept any double standard in this regard under any circumstances. Thus we can see the greatness of a man named M. Fethullah Gülen, a religious preacher, author, thinker, philosopher, and poet from Anatolia, who has become rightfully renowned all over the world for his tireless activities dedicated to the genuine revival of Islamic values based on the common understanding and heritage of humankind.

CHAPTER 1

Gülen Echoes Rumi with a Difference

GÜLEN ECHOES RUMI WITH A DIFFERENCE

The worst of scholars are those who visit princes, and the best of princes are those who visit scholars. Wise is the prince who stands at the door of the poor, and wretched are the poor who stand at the door of the prince.

Rumi

Man has a responsibility to show compassion to all living beings, as a requirement of being human. The more he displays compassion, the more exalted he becomes, while the more he resorts to wrongdoing, oppression and cruelty, the more he is disgraced and humiliated, becoming a shame to humanity.

Fethullah Gülen

In the writings of Jalaluddin Rumi (1207–1273), who saw the acme of happiness in suffering for the beloved, the gap between comfort and unease is only a narrow one. Such love has very little place now in modern life. The meaning of sacrifice and suffering for love is missing in the urban mindset in almost all highly industrialized societies, and many find it undignified to play the role of lover wholeheartedly without being loved more in return. In this sense, Fethullah Gülen has attempted to expand the modern social space for selfless love and sacrifice for all humanity in general and for his fellow citizens in particular with a special emphasis on common human dignity. Religious, social, and cultural responsibilities go hand in hand in Gülen's thought.

It is notable that Rumi did not play any politics with Islamic tenets or doctrines. For Rumi, the entire life of a believer is mysterious, and only a committed and dedicated soul can unlock some of the hidden mysteries in life to make use of them for the betterment of others. In much of Rumi's thought, material life is insignificant for the cultural and spiritual journey one has to undergo in this world. The spiritual and cultural dimensions of human life have a deep impact on the social setting, which is supported and protected by political doctrines and economic theories that are, for their part, well-nourished through state mechanisms.

Rumi's appreciation and upholding of spiritual essence of human dignity has not been fully understood in many Eastern and Western societies, where genuine people's voices are either too complicated to be heard or too low to be taken care of. It is no wonder it took so long (about 800 years) for many Muslims as well to truly appreciate Rumi's calling and yearning for spirituality for all, irrespective of race, religion, and gender.

Gülen's explanations of the religious and spiritual dimensions of human life and society are also clear and all-inclusive. "People today must be relieved from social, political, cultural, economic, and various other depressions that are bending them over double, forcing their back into a misshapen twisted form...The morality of our attitudes and actions is directly related to the consciousness of responsibility, which has been idealized in our spirits."[1]

Immoral activities and attitudes are not incidental outcomes of the social or cultural life of a state or community. We can talk about cultural revolution endlessly, but to bring about a sustainable cultural change and keep that change compatible with the inherent values of a religious or non-religious society is not an easy task. Political and social reformers of all kinds have struggled hard to bring about successful cultural revolutions and to change the economic values of a society or community. In the early days of Islam, we saw a widespread tribal revolt against the proposed cultural and economic changes put forward by the Prophet of Islam. Along with the initial message of Divine Unity, much of the core message of Islam occupied the societal and cultural domain and was a serious and comprehensive attempt to change the entire worldview of tribal people for whom blood relation is the determining factor in establishing, breaking, and destroying all other relationships and communications.

Some historians have claimed that Prophet Muhammad, peace and blessings be upon him, tried to build an Arab nation based on the unity of Arab tribes living in and around the cities of Mecca and Medina. One may find that argument very convincing in terms of reforms undertaken and carried out successfully by the Prophet of Islam and his Companions. However, if we analyze the core message of Islam and visions of the Islamic caliphate, we can barely find any attempts at nation-building in the prophetic mission of Islam.

However, it often appears that the political objectives of Islam are more dominant than its cultural and economic mission. Throughout Islamic history and Muslim civilization, Muslims have periodically failed Islam politically and economically, but Islam has survived culturally, and its influence on the hearts and minds of the people still remains a mystery, and its spiritual appeal is becoming stronger day by day around the globe.

This phenomenal influence over people in shaping and reshaping their lives throughout the fourteen-century history of Islam cannot have been the work of one person or nation alone. However, from time to time, this missionary work had to be led, especially when Muslim nations were caught in political or economic crisis. Rumi's creativity occurred at a period of severe crisis in Muslim political history, but he wanted Muslims to be more concerned about adhering to civility and humility in the exercise of their religious and moral duties.

Rumi was very focused on individual spiritual salvation, while Gülen is very concerned about how to raise the level of collective consciousness to achieve the objective of society-building, and this objective is not limited to Anatolia. Of course, Sufism at its core has always been a very peaceful movement to purify the individual heart and mind and to make a person dedicated to the cause of magnifying the "Islamic blessing" for all, irrespective of race, religion, or creed. Even so, secular Turkey has found Sufism intolerable and thus *tariqas*, or Sufi religious orders, were banned in 1926.

None of the prominent Muslim rulers of the twentieth century recognized fully that Sufis would persist with their peace-loving efforts under any circumstances. In the 1980s, however, the Turkish ruling elite realized that truth and enacted a change in governmental behavior towards Sufi groups in Turkey. Under the leadership of Turgut Özal,[2] the Turkish governmental attitude toward the Gülen movement changed and the government stopped persecuting people for simple religious charitable activities.

Rumi never witnessed such a sea of change in governmental attitudes toward Sufi activities and thought. In Gülen's time, we have seen a huge change in the relationship between governmentally endorsed religious activities and religiously motivated charitable works handled by individual citizens and groups. However, when it comes to purifying the individual soul, both Rumi and Gülen speak from a similar perspective. A distinctive feature of Gülen's worldview is that it cannot be characterized as completely secular or religious.

> By means of scientific thinking and understanding, as we realized long ago, long before the West did, we must immerse and imbue our younger generations with science and ideas, and thus realize our revival, our Renaissance....The Universe is a book which is displayed by the Creator before the eyes of man to be referred to frequently. Man is a lens open to observe the depths of existence, and a transparent index of all worlds. Life is a manifestation, the assumption of forms, of the meanings which are filtered from that book and index, and is the reflection of that which reverberates from Divine discourse.[3]

One can easily observe here that Gülen speaks like a modern Rumi. Though Rumi did not have the luxury of modern science and technology, he could visualize the unfolding methods of natural sciences through the intellectual exercise of the human brain and actions. According to Gülen, Rumi had "the enthusiasm and excitement"[4] to seek for the truth whether its shape or form is tangible or not. Gülen has given Rumi a different voice that attempts to bring the latter's spirituality closer to social reformers and activists. Such an approach makes Gülen a unique author and preacher not only from the Turkish perspective, but also on the global stage. The Turkish secular environment was not impossible to negotiate for Gülen because his mature ideas made his intellectual avenues broader and not hostile to secular circles.

How can Gülen walk such a fine line in his presentation of Islam as a mission of comprehensive social reform? Philosophically articulating Islam as a world vision for the whole of humanity, Gülen's call to all Muslims to become better human beings is very appealing. Instead of causing discomfort in atheists or Muslim secularists about Islamic ideas of social reform, Gülen has shown great sensitivity towards Turkish secular regimes as well as religious groups that are engaged in making the Turkish nation more "Islamic."[5]

Like Rumi, Gülen is fully aware of the danger of the politicization of Islamic ideas of polity and socio-political reforms. On the other hand, Gülen is bold enough to say that without Islamic ideas, no Muslim nation or society can undertake any serious plan to reshape their society in the present environment of science and technology. Without showing appropriate respect to the Muslim masses, their rulers cannot implement any political, economic, or social reforms successfully. Unlike in the West where a separation of "church and state" often persists, it is a reality that most people in the Muslim world see their religion, Islam, as very relevant to their material life as well. Anyone interested in reforming a Muslim state or society must take this special feature of Muslim nations into account.

Mistakenly it was believed that with the process of industrialization and urbanization, Muslim nations would become as agnostic or atheistic as North American or European societies. Turkey is one of the most industrialized countries in the Muslim world. However, Turkey has been becoming more "Islamic" at greater speed in recent decades than many other Muslim countries. Nevertheless, this does not mean that Turkey has abandoned its constitutional principles of secularism and nationalism, which are apparently at loggerheads with "Political Islam."

Secularism without atheistic indoctrination is quite acceptable to Islamic values that promote interfaith dialogue and the utmost respect for the followers of other religions and non-believers. Gülen has been attempting to explain Islamic values and principles without provoking any secular quarter that might take him as a threat to the establishment. His approach to the establishment is that if it is to be pro-people, it has to listen to the voice of Islam and the people at the same time as they are intertwined through many cultural and societal channels. Rumi's emphasis was on creating more channels of communication between people with a deeper compassion for others, while Gülen is more interested in implementing or using those channels to bring educational and social reforms.

Rumi tried to reduce the gap between '*ulama* Islam' and folk Islam. Rumi communicates many things, multiple meanings, at many levels, simultaneously; he provides explanations and keys to unlock the meaning of reality; all the words, all the stories and explanations he conveyed say nothing more than reality, which has been expressed so far by all the great masters of the *tasawwuf* tradition in Islam. He communicated through the power of literature what he learned from the *madrasah* to the hearts of the people around him, as well as the religious and political elite. Rumi's *Mathnawi* is for both well-educated people and people with little education.[6]

BRIDGING THE GAPS AND EMBRACING HUMANITY

In his famous couplet, "*We are like a pair of compasses, while one leg stands firm on the Islamic Law, the other travels the seventy-two nations,*" Rumi advised Muslims to keep one leg firmly in the center of the Islamic belief system and try to travel other faiths and the non-Islamic world with the other. For Rumi, none of the seventy-two sects which people follow in approaching Islam and the Qur'an

is untouchable because followers of all those sects can be incorporated within one universal spiritual system called *tasawwuf.*

Muslim critics of Rumi are very harsh on him for these liberal
views and many of them have called him a polluter of genuine
Islamic beliefs. Some critics have argued that Rumi had deliberate-
ly cast himself out of the orbit of Islam. It is believed that on one
occasion Rumi said, "I am not a Christian, a Jew, a Zoroastrian, or
a Muslim." To his critics, this is evidence of Rumi's disbelief, and
so he could be regarded as a non-Muslim. Was it a blunder on the
part of Rumi to say that he was not even a Muslim in the traditional sense? Not at all! Criticizing the followers of different religions
and their arrogant practices, Rumi wanted to say that he was not
practicing any extreme kind of religiosity.

Nonetheless, to prove himself a devout Muslim, Rumi wrote:

> I am the servant of the Qur'an as long as I have life.
> I am the dust on the path of Muhammad, the Chosen one.
> If anyone quotes anything except this from my sayings,
> I am quit of him and outraged by those words.

Professor Eric Geoffrey is absolutely correct when he says that
"most Western sources took Mevlana [Rumi] out of the context of
his Islamic roots."[7] Neither Rumi nor Gülen has maintained tunnel
vision of any Islamic tenets or values, which are at their core humanistic and universal so as to accommodate the whole of humankind within the orbit of *tasawwuf.* Having a great affection for the
creation because of the Creator, they see the entire creation as a
manifestation of divine Attributes. While not putting anything
worldly in the heart, they love everything, at the same time, not just
for themselves but for the remembrance of God. Abandoning the
world in their hearts but not physically, they are concerned about
everyone, aiming to embrace people from all walks of life without
seeking anything worldly in return. As Elisabeth Özdalga notes,

> Gülen's views have little to do with seeking political power or
> even traditional Islam but rather have more in common with

Max Weber's ideas about "worldly asceticism." The perspective taught by Gülen is based on activism, stirred up, as well as controlled, by pietism. This "activist pietism" (or Weber's "in-worldly asceticism") describes a new feature in Turkish religious life. In accordance with Weber's analysis of in-worldly asceticism, the general effect of Gülen's similar "activist pietism" has also been in the direction of a rationalization of social relationships. In conformity with Weber's concept, Gülen's "pietistic activism" is based on a critical "rejection of the world" but not the "flight from this world" that is characteristic for escapist mysticism.[8]

Max Weber (1864–1920) was not a mystic; he was a non-Marxist thinker with a mind to accept religious and cultural values at a time when believing in religion in Europe had already become unfashionable and Turkish secularism was being deeply influenced by anti-Islamic thought. Weber emerged as the foremost specialist in the sociology of religion and government, and successfully conceptualized religious and ethical behavior in economic and political activities.

> Gülen-inspired educators seem to be acting out a form of "piety through work," similar to the Protestant ethic observed by Max Weber. Exemplifying the civil/cosmopolitan form, Gülen-inspired teachers act in accordance with Gülen's teachings, treating faith as a matter of personal religiousness. Civic engagement is viewed as an external expression of that religiousness in the form of dedication, diligence, hard work, and service.[9]

For European and Western analysts, it is mostly through this kind of approach to Islamic activism that they try to appreciate the Gülen movement for education, spiritual enlightenment, and a civil state under the rule of universal morality. It is typically difficult for Westerners to truly appreciate many nuances of Islamic activism for civil decency and spiritual salvation. With the process of European Christian values becoming more liberal, atheism was the natural destiny for most Europeans. The works of Marx and Engels were a reflection of the ongoing dispute between Christian forces and the atheistic orientation of socialism and capitalism. It is to be noted that Max Weber wanted to neutralize the extreme atheistic propaganda that had swept through the whole of Europe and which did not offer an activism that could change society based on ethics and universal morality and human dignity.

GÜLEN'S APPROACH TO ISLAMIC SPIRITUAL LIFE

The Sufi way of living has been misinterpreted by many ultra-orthodox and dogmatic circles around the Muslim world, and it is also true that some Muslims without doing their part to change their conditions, just hope for an easy life and happiness in this world and the hereafter. Gülen belongs to neither of these groups. His spirituality is based on an interpretation of the Qur'an and Islam that promotes active service to humanity and society as a spiritual practice. He has no record of any passivity nor any history of destructive thought in his sermons in his career as a preacher and prolific Islamic author over a period of five decades. All along he has been a devout Muslim and social activist, thinker, and religious preacher with a deep knowledge of all the nuances of Islam. In some contemporary *tariqa*s (Sufi orders), passivity is taught as a way of life, and many Muslims simply believe that just by having good faith in one's heart, one can achieve any height of spirituality and worldly happiness.

To Gülen, if a particular interpretation of Islam is unable to cure the social and economic diseases of a society, then that interpretation should have little value to Muslims as believers who should be dedicating their entire lives to the betterment of society. In accomplishing this duty toward society or their fellow human beings, Muslims should not be driven by a self-righteous attitude or agenda. It is in this belief that we find the basis of Gülen's liberal approach toward Qur'anic principles or interpretations. However, Gülen is very careful not to break any enduring religious tradition, even if a specific practice long observed is not of Islamic import. Gülen is a modern man who does not adorn himself with any Islamic symbols, but he has never shown any hostility toward the traditional behavior of

Muslims. As a result, his endorsement of the religious piety upheld by Ghazali or Rumi is categorical and does not bring any suspicion to the minds of ordinary Muslim men and women.

Gülen is not opportunist in his dialogue with people of other religions or civilizations. His love and compassionate attitude toward humans facilitates genuine interaction and dialogue between people of different faiths. Gülen believes in peaceful co-existence with others with the common goal of building a decent human society. In order to achieve that goal, everyone should be accepted as they are without being required to give up their own religious or moral principles. Like Rumi, Gülen is also very strong in his belief that a true spiritual and religious act has its own intrinsic value for the actor and any others who are in touch with him or her.

To Gülen, human dignity and genuine spirituality are inseparable from the human soul, which tends to crave the higher truth and greater fulfillment of human existence on earth. The spiritual heights that can be achieved by the human soul are unlimited, and thus no one can claim any superiority over others in piety or human dignity. In Muslim communities, a serious problem can arise when people try to determine the degree of truth or falsehood in the religiosity of a Muslim man or woman. As Arif comments,

> Rumi... digs deeply into the morality which shapes society's ethics through questioning its utility and application. His careful insights, developed through detailed analysis and synthesis, not only enlighten us about the pitfalls of certain thinking patterns and the faulty behaviors which emerge as a result, but also provide us with the remedy and guidance to correct what is wrong in order to adapt to what is right. In this way, he does not admonish us, in effect, but simply relates the enigmas and paradoxes of life, to strengthen our souls so that we might resist and repel all that is unnatural, impure, and thus, inhuman.[10]

Without changing society from its core, no substantial sociopolitical or economic reform can be sustainable for a long period of time. The core values of a society are a combination of many ingrained phenomena that have been inherited from diverse sources—the religio-cultural system, customs, economic paradigms, so-cio-political values, and so on. Rumi's contribution is very varied and invaluable in many areas of both humanism and Islam. We can take a fresh look at Rumi even today in the twenty-first century. What is the secret of Rumi's contribution to the universal ideals of Islam and humanism in general?

Rumi collected the treasures of the Islamic civilization that had accumulated during seventh to twelfth centuries in his writings and spiritual activities. He lived through Islam's longest political crisis in the thirteenth century and was never frustrated or demoralized by the rise and fall of Muslim rulers. Rumi was concerned with the fundamental causes of the evolution of human societies through the prisms of ethics and spirituality. Rumi's world of creativity and the spiritual domain is subjective because it depends on the creative power of the Creator, God Almighty, but it is also objective be-cause of its mundane character that draws on the rational activities of human beings.

Rumi did not want to undermine perceptions of the role and place of God and human beings on earth or in the heavens as the ho-rizons of human activity overlap with the many creative directions of the unseen God, Who remains at the center of Rumi's thought pat-terns. Rumi's yearning to discover more mysteries on Earth was like a heavenly task for an individual to come to know the real spirit of the human soul and its journey to heaven. This never-ending quest for genuine humanism requires vigorous searching of one's own soul to achieve integration with the humanness of the whole of human-kind. As Dinorshoyev nicely captures it,

> For that reason Rumi propagated loving relations with Greeks, Arabs, Turks, Europeans, that is, with all people of all different religions and creeds. In this regard Rumi was fully convinced that God Almighty is a unique integrated whole for all mankind, but ways to Him are many. Any thought con-trary to this universal ideal may lead to animosity between the people of different religions and may create confusion leading to fanaticism. According to Rumi the central theme here is to

determine the role and place of human beings on earth as active peacemakers between people of all races and socio-economic situations sustained by the different political systems of all the corners of the planet that make every human being equal in the eyes of God. To achieve this ultimate goal of humanism, God's Will is to bring people together in dialogue for the sake of the preservation of humankind with all its diversity in culture and civilization.[11]

Eight hundred years ago, Rumi could see the main problem of modern human beings, who are still bewildered in their relations with their fellow humans. The cornerstone of Rumi's spiritual teaching was that we are on earth to unite people, not to divide them. The Prophet of Islam united many Arab tribes under the banner of Islam and very quickly the Arabs, for the first time in human history, emerged as a nation. Though early Muslims transformed their city state of Medina into an empire governed by the caliph of Islam within a short period of time, they never tried to create a state exclusively for Arabs or Muslims. The concept of the caliphate is a kind of super state that has almost no similarity with a nation state. Throughout the entire period of the rise of nation-statehood, Muslims were divided over the issue of caliphate, but the nation state is ultimately one of the outcomes of colonialism.

Turkey escaped the typical Muslim experience of European colonization. Under European colonial rule Muslim nations were under tremendous pressure to abandon much of their Islamic and Muslim heritage. From the later decades of the nineteenth century, the Ottoman Turks was also caught up in a nationalistic fervor that ultimately turned into aggressive secularism. This does not mean that all kinds of Islamic phenomena and the traditional Muslim way of life were completely abandoned in Turkey under the various types of secular regime that ruled there in the twentieth century. Moreover, Turks as a people largely escaped the full effects of atheistic socialism or communism. According to Rumi, all wars are either meaningless or foolish. What about ideological wars? Rumi offers many answers to this question as well. Rumi's answers are full of love, compassion, and respect for others. Fethullah Gülen is in fact a modern Rumi of Turkey with a distinct voice calling for interfaith and intra-civilizational dialogue.

Like Rumi, Gülen also finds two distinct categories of people in the Muslim community, dividing them into *kitabi* Islam (any group that follows some kind of revealed text strictly) and *ummi*, or popular, Islam.[12] Since the early decades of the nineteenth century, this division has become stronger and sharper. Many Muslim communities have been trying to figure out how to live out the real mission of the Prophet of Islam and many have become confused by too strong a focus on the outer manifestation of the ritual obligations of Muslims. The quarrel between the secularists in Muslim countries and Islamists of all kinds did not help to resolve this problem. While Muslims were having difficulties in adequately describing their Prophet as a politician, peacemaker, and social reformer, scholars with other religious backgrounds came up with excellent descriptions of Prophet Muhammad, peace and blessings be upon him. Mahatma Gandhi, for instance, said,

> I become more than ever convinced that it was not the sword that won a place for Islam in those days in the scheme for life. It was the rigid simplicity, the utter self-effacement of the Prophet, the scrupulous regard for his pledges, his intense devotion to his friends and followers, his intrepidity, his fearlessness, his absolute trust in God and his own mission. These and not the sword, carried everything before them and surmounted every trouble. The sayings of Muhammad are a treasure of wisdom not only for Muslims but for all mankind.[13]

Time and again, during the crisis period of the Muslims, many exponents of *kitabi* Islam have forgotten that the Qur'an, Islam or the Prophet are not the treasure of wisdom or the way of life only for this or that group of Muslims, but rather these resources are open to the whole of humankind and anybody can benefit from them with some kind of belief in Islam. Eight hundred years ago, Rumi reminded Muslims of this, and in the twenty-first century we are receiving a similar message in Gülen's thoughts and ideas of personal and social reform. It is not an easy task to comprehend fully that the Gülen movement is indeed a comprehensive spiritual and social movement at the same time. In this regard it is rather difficult to distinguish between Rumi and Gülen. However, it is too early to tell what legacy Gülen will leave behind for us. It appears that Gülen has no interest in political activity and does not intend to have any Sufi order of his own. In this too, it is not easy to find a difference between Rumi and Gülen.

Dinorshoyev notes the following:

> In the development of Muslim mystic wisdom, the foremost contribution of Jalaluddin Rumi is that he had successfully combined the theoretical aspects of mysticism with their importance in establishing unity among different kinds of *tariqas*. For modern human beings, it is important that social and humanitarian sciences of the day can find right answers to the problem inherent in his system of mysticism to be solved by men... Poems of Rumi received wide attention just after they were translated by Ryukerta. Just by reading the translation of Ryukerta, the famous German philosopher, Hegel, immediately could recognize in Rumi the superb philosophical mysticism and poetic gift that has been mentioned in his "Ascetic" and "Philosophical Soul."[14]

Translations of the works of Gülen have started to appear in the West, and we have to wait to see how Western authors review and evaluate Gülen as a contemporary Rumi. However, we can say for sure that Gülen is neither a traditional Muslim scholar nor a Sufi of a particular *tariqa*, and he combines many basic qualities of a jurist and preacher of *umma*ite (world) class. Traditional *ulama* (Islamic scholars) of our time simply preserve information from Islamic sources and narrate it when they are asked to do so. Some authors call them "conveyors"[15] of Islamic resources.

In this modern information age, these conveyors can play little role in solving any important problem Muslims have been suffering from. However, every Muslim country has numerous conveyors of

Islam and Muslim culture who are incapable of giving leadership in the ongoing reform of their societies. As a result, among the Muslim elite many were excited to see authors like Mawdudi and Qutb and believed that they might fulfill the need of the day. It is a fact that these modern exponents of Islamic ideology based on a religio-political culture intended to restore Islam in their own countries at any cost. Here also Gülen is an exception to the general phenomenon in the present-day Muslim world. Gülen does not forget the situation of his homeland, but his vision of the revival of Islamic spirituality has a much wider focus than the rise of political Islam in some particular Muslim country. Ali Bulaç, one of the prominent Islamic thinkers in Turkey, writes:

> While he [Gülen] can analyze a *hadith* meticulously in terms of authenticity, he is simultaneously able to manifest his interpretations on current issues. This new leader type uses the canonical sources of the Qur'an and the Sunna, and has a good knowledge of Islamic sciences and Islamic history, along with contemporary science and current developments. In fact, a leader's efficacy diminishes when either of these characteristics is lacking, as in the case of the current Turkish *ulama*, who are cut off from the contemporary world, and Turkish intellectuals, who know nothing about Islam and history.[16]

The rise of political Islam is a serious dilemma faced by most of contemporary Muslim countries and communities, and it stimulated the rise of extremism and fanaticism in many parts of the world where colonial powers found it easier to implement a policy of "divide and rule." Gülen has not taken sides in the feud in the Muslim world between secularists and Islamists who are locked in an ideological battle over the control of the rotten state machinery left behind by the European colonizers.

While we claim that Gülen echoes Rumi in preaching universal peace and harmony for all based on a deeper understanding of Islamic tenets, we would like to add that many of us are not fully aware of the enormity of the task of reforming our societies and communities in line with inherent (*fitrah*) human values.

CHAPTER 2

Sufism in Theory and Practice:
Gülen's Perspective

SUFISM IN THEORY AND PRACTICE:
GÜLEN'S PERSPECTIVE

S ufism can simply be described as the spiritual dimension of the Islamic way of life, or in the words of Gülen, it is "the spiritual life of Islam."[1] There are various terms that are currently in use for Sufism, including *tasawwuf*, the Sufi Way, Islamic spirituality, and Islamic mysticism. Putting emphasis on the spiritual aspect of Islam and unlike "political" Islam, Sufism is mainly concerned with the enrichment of the inner world of human beings on their journey to the Absolute Truth, and it usually but not necessarily brings people under one or other of the different *tariqa* or Sufi religious orders, that is, under a spiritual umbrella for co-worshippers.

It is necessary to point out here that a person can truly be transformed and spiritually uplifted through the works and talks of spiritual masters. However, one's joining of the religious gatherings of spiritual teachers or benefiting from the works of such men of God for one's own spiritual journey to the Absolute Truth does not necessarily mean that there has to be a Sufi order which one follows or that people must be *murid*s, or disciples, of a certain Sufi sheikh. The core of the issue is that one benefits greatly from the works or gatherings that take place in the spiritual presence of true saints or spiritual masters who have experience of the heart while journeying on the spiritual path toward God, as Rumi stated beautifully in a couplet: "My heart, be seated near that person who has experience of the heart / Go under that tree which bears fresh blossoms."[2]

Gülen points out that "sainthood marked with sincere friendship of God is the best of sainthood."[3] Saints can feel sincere friendship with God according to their capacity and rank. Therefore, although all the saints are people of deep spirituality who have obtained God's special nearness, they have a limit to their perfectibility according to their capacity. A saint may be distinguished from others by particular virtues in which he or she may excel others:

> [The saints or friends of God] differ in disposition and temperament, in their degree of attainment, and in their duties and missions. This is why they are mentioned with different titles such as *abrar* (the godly, the virtuous ones), *muqarrabun* (those favored with God's special nearness), *abdal* (substitutes), *nujaba* (nobles), *nukaba* (custodians), *awtad* (pillars), *ghawth* (helpers or means of divine help), and *qutb* (poles). Whatever title they are called, all of them have—according to the capacity of each— common praiseworthy qualities such as truthfulness, honesty, trustworthiness, sincerity and purity of intention, piety, righteousness, abstinence, asceticism, and so on. And with the exception of a few extreme "ecstatics" among them, all of them act within the bounds of Islamic principles.[4]

Gülen has been very cautious with regard to the practice of some sections of the Muslim world that give disproportionate attention to ritualism at the expense of the broader universal teachings of Islam and to the positions of some Sufis who do not comply with the traditions directly derived from the tenets of Islam and who have thus regressed, misleading both themselves and others. However, Gülen has never dismissed the role and importance of Sufi orders in the Muslim world, particularly during the rise and fall of civilizations:

> Although some Sufis were fanatic adherents of their own ways, and some religious scholars (i.e., legal scholars, Traditionists, and interpreters of the Qur'an) did restrict themselves to the outer dimension of religion, those who follow and represent the middle, straight path have always formed the majority.[5]

Today, many leading circles of many different societies and religions do not consider mainstream Muslim thought to offer a way of life or system of nation- and state-building. In isolation from political and economic predicaments, foundational religious issues of Islam are quite easy to explain. However, placing these issues in a particular national and economic context and applying them in the material realities of life is very challenging. Moreover, Muslims tend to dispute the legitimacy of various Sufi orders within the parameters of jurisprudence as presented in books of *fiqh*, or the science of the application of Islamic jurisprudence. Indeed, both in the past and the present, Sufism has been handled in works by Muslims in both positive and negative ways. The difference of opinion, especially on many *tariqa*-related issues, is vast among the traditional *ulama* (scholars) and orthodox religious circles, and there are even some jurists who do not see any rightful place for Sufi orders among the four main schools of jurisprudence of Islam.

Gülen wants to free his readers of any prejudices or pre-conceived confusions about Sufism as the spiritual aspect of Islam and its relation to the different schools of jurisprudence. He has written a series of four books on Sufism that provides comprehensive coverage of the general ideas and practices of spirituality at different stages in Muslim history under different schools of theological discourse. Gülen's *Emerald Hills of the Heart: Key Concepts in the Practice of Sufism* series is a monumental work on the spiritual dimension of Islamic thought and life. *Emerald Hills of the Heart* presents a horizon and a goal that needs to be reached and shows the paths to leaving the animal state, abandoning attachments to the physical and material, and rising to the vital degrees of the heart and spirit.

While he elucidates clearly the fundamentals and different aspects of Islamic spiritual life in his four-volume work, Gülen does not support any particular Sufi order as such nor does he propagate a new *tariqa*, or path, in any way or form. Instead, he provides the contemporary audience clear descriptions for a whole range of different issues of Sufism.

A reader may wonder why Gülen has gone into so much in detail about the different terms of Sufism and its different manifestations in group practice and individual piety. Gülen has a clear answer to this:

> As a religion, Islam naturally emphasizes the spiritual realm. It takes the training of the ego as a basic principle. Asceticism, piety, kindness and sincerity are essential to it. In the history of Islam the discipline that dwelt most on such matters was Sufism.[6]

In his work, Gülen articulates "the spiritual life of Islam from within a conceptual framework, which rather than perceiving Sufism as an intangible science with peculiar concepts, envisages Sufism as the spiritual facet of Islam, or simply spiritual life per se."[7] Gülen presents Sufi concepts within the boundaries and limits of the Islamic measures and the enormous profundity and infinity of spiritual life:

> For spiritual or Sufi life to advance on the basis of Islamic principles or along the guidelines of Islamic jurisprudence without causing or suffering any digressions, it [the four-volume work of Gülen on Sufism] delineates the limits of the spiritual path, illuminating it at the same time with floodlit projectors that it has placed at every stage and station. While sketching such limits, at the same time it destroys all limits and borders imposed before the spiritual journeying.[8]

Gülen emphasizes Sufism's practical aspect rather than its institutionalized forms in his *Emerald Hills of the Heart: Key Concepts in the Practice of Sufism* series. In this respect, the series is an essential, detailed guide to "the Islamic spiritual life that constitutes the core of Islam not as a theoretical subject but as lived by the Companions of the Prophet. It presents this life as a profound experience of the heart, mind, and body described and appointed by Islam. It also investigates how it has taken shape throughout history. Gülen's *Emerald Hills of the Heart: Key Concepts in the Practice of Sufism* series bequeaths to future ages the legacy of Sufism with all its dimensions, or the spiritual life of Islam, in its immense entirety as a safe and sound road that has been protected against all manner of deviations."[9]

THE QUEST FOR THE ORIGINAL SUFISM

Despite theoretical differences of opinion between Muslim jurists and Sufis over legal and quasi-legal issues concerning the interpretation of the sources of Islamic jurisprudence, those disputes have few implications for the practical life of a Muslim. Indeed, Sufism as the spiritual dimension of the Islamic way of life can never be thought of as independent of Islamic jurisprudence. Gülen makes this point very clear: "In fact, Sufism and jurisprudence are like the two colleges of a university that seeks to teach its students the two dimensions of the *shari'a*, enabling them to practice it in their daily lives."[10] "It is a distortion to present the viewpoints of Sufis and the thoughts and conclusions of *shari'a* scholars as essentially different from each other."[11]

Sufism, in the words of Gülen, "is based on observing even the most 'trivial' rules of the *Shari'a* in order to penetrate their inner meaning."[12] For Gülen, *shari'a*, or the set of the rules and laws established by the Qur'an and Sunna, and Sufism, or the inner dimension of the *shari'a*, must not be separated from each other:

> An initiate or traveler on the path (*salik*) never separates the outer observance of the Shari'ah from its inner dimension, and therefore observes all of the requirements of both the outer and the inner dimensions of Islam. Through such observance, he or she travels toward the goal in utmost humility and submission.[13]

Sufism, in this sense, enables Muslims to internalize Islamic faith and practice by moving beyond simply obeying the Divine commands and performing acts of worship without much attention to their interior transformative power as this would result in disproportionate attention to ritualism alone.

It is a serious intellectual challenge to establish that the jurists and Sufis can work together with the same kinds of religious and worldly objectives side by side to promote a universal system of justice and welfare-oriented governance. Islam can be taken as a way of learning, thinking, and living at the same time. Thus, it is a complex problem for any Islamic activist and preacher to build a common platform for all the different kinds of Muslims with different historical, cultural, and economic backgrounds.

For Gülen, these differences are not at all a fundamental issue as all Muslims are supposed to follow the universal principles of Islamic jurisprudence and live an Islamic spiritual life at the same time. However, not every Muslim or even every nation is capable of accommodating all the diverse ideas of the different spiritual paths or *tariqa*s in their religious and mundane activities. Gülen advocates a method of making every Muslim part of a religious and spiritual revival all over the world, and his orientation has been like that of Muslim saints and *mujtahids*[14] of earlier generations.

In popular perception, the *awliya* (God's friends or saints) are different than the *mujtahids*. It is believed that some saints do not follow any structured methodology prescribed directly by God's words, while *mujtahids* are strict in their ways of living in accordance with the injunctions of Islamic law. In reality, however, the saints' scrupulous observance of God's commandments and God's taking them under His special care and protection in return are the two dimensions of true sainthood.

When discussing the fact that Sufism has been defined in many ways, Gülen refers to the claims that the term "Sufi" is related to the words *sof* (wool), *safa* (spiritual delight, exhilaration), *safwa* (purity), and so on. Regarding the origin of Sufism, he clearly expresses that Sufism is the spiritual dimension of the Islamic way of life and opposes the idea that it is derived from the word *sophos* (a Greek word meaning wisdom), saying that "this is a fabrication of foreign researchers who try to prove that Sufism has a foreign—and therefore non-Islamic—origin."[15]

If someone does not have any inclination to spirituality, then he or she can lead a life of his or her own without any specific spiritual goals. However, for believers or true Muslims, the issue of intention occupies the central place in all activities throughout their entire lives. A true believer does not take any credit or pride in doing good works as the religious principle teaches that one's doing righteous deeds is a responsibility and a divine blessing.

Some Sufis use the maxim, "Die before you die!" to control their ego and to nourish their heart and souls with a higher degree of humility and a sense of responsibility to treat others better in preference to their own self interest. A materialist view would suggest that this is a kind of self humiliation that would ultimately prove to be detrimental to the material prosperity of society as a whole. Gülen takes the Sufi view that it is a sign of the enlightenment of the human soul ultimately leading to the emancipation of the entire society in all its aspects. According to Gülen, the spiritual life of Sufism is fundamentally different than the presumed pre-Islamic roots of philosophers' thoughts on austerity or complete isolation of individuals from societal or state affairs:

> Prior to Islam, some Hindu and Greek philosophers followed various ways leading to self-purification and struggled against their carnal desires and the attractions of the world. But Sufism is essentially different from these ways. For example, Sufis live their entire lives as a quest to purify their selves via invocation, regular worship, complete obedience to God, self-control, and humility, whereas ancient philosophers did not observe any of these rules or acts.[16]

Prior to the rise of Islamic civilization, one could not find so many religious, spiritual, and cultural ways to keep oneself free of arrogance and ignorance either based on superstition or ego-related complexes. Different religious orders have attempted to formulate various means to save Muslims from greed, selfishness, jealousy, and cruel attitudes and the craving for worldly happiness and different types of immorality on earth. Deep down, every human soul wishes to accomplish a much higher goal than merely to eat, drink, and then die like any other lesser form of life. This is why the question of happiness is so important for every human being. The discernment and knowledge of creation, life, right and wrong, and of the Divine system prevailing in the universe is important in order to find persuasive answers to questions such as how to find genuine happiness on earth, how to make one's sense of immortality meaningful, and how to see the higher causes in life beyond one's selfish interests and so on. These are only some of the issues Sufis concentrate upon.

The Qur'an is the source of knowledge in all these vital matters. According to Gülen, *hikma* (wisdom) accompanies this main source of knowledge. Accordingly, the Sunna of the Prophet, the system or principles by which to understand and practice revealed knowledge in daily life, comes to mind first of all when speaking of *hikma* (the wisdom of the Prophet). Referring to the verse of the Qur'an: *"Call to the way of your Lord with wisdom and fair exhortation and preaching,"*[17] Gülen says that the Islamic "wisdom means the subtleties and mysteries of the Qur'an."[18] His understanding is that wisdom "with its theoretical and practical aspects, means good will" both in individual and communal life spreading all over the world. Based on this understanding of Islam, Gülen has advised the entire Turkish people to spread out all over the world to talk about and teach good will. He also warns that in this regard no sentiment of nationalism or extremism should play any role in Turkish people's service to humanity and volunteerism as a part of universal human dignity. Here the important lesson to be learned is that everybody should do good works competing with each other as if in a race without being much concerned about the outcome or consequence of hard work for the wellbeing of a nation or humankind.

Regarding the employment of useful knowledge and righteous deeds in combination in practical life, Gülen notes, "Righteous deeds are the willed outcome of knowledge applied, and the beginning of new Divine gifts" and advises "giving everything its due, or right judgment, without going to extremes, viewing and discharging our responsibilities in the framework of the Islamic law."[19]

Here we find Gülen's superb understanding of the practicality of Sufism and law, which may, I think, provide the framework for good socioeconomic and legal systems rather than offering Islamic law as an alternative to a codified legal system. Islamic law established by the Divine Book and the Prophetic Traditions may provide a blueprint for good governance as a system of law. It can serve as a basis for but not an alternative to either civil or common law-based judicial systems. A functional legal and judicial system needs strong public morality and a law-abiding mentality which is widespread and deep-rooted among the public and without which even the mandatory rules and regulations are mere "black letters of law." The transnational character of Islamic law has been misunderstood in many quarters including by many Islamic scholars. There are many people who believe that a system of nation states is not compatible with universal Islamic ideals and cannot have a legitimate existence under Islamic law. Many Muslims fail to appreciate the fact that present-day nation states are a reality in the global context and a legacy of colonialism that we cannot simply ignore. We need to make these existing states more welfare-oriented so that the majority can benefit from them.

Muslims simply cannot ignore the reality of international life and the global economic order that dictates and determines many of the dynamics of national life under the nation state system. It is difficult to serve the noble ideals of Islamic values and governance within the nation state system. However, ignoring the reality of this system would be arrogant behavior toward neighboring states or could even be detrimental to the ideals of Islam and cause ultra-nationalist feelings to rise. Moreover, such an attitude might be detrimental to the economic interests of any nation. Still some great powers play the national card in international politics and do not respect the sovereignty of others. Some Muslim scholars are very confused about the concepts of the Sovereignty of Almighty-God over the entire universe and state sovereignty; they think that a Muslim nation state can have a perfect Islamic constitution.[20] However, there is no doubt that the sources of Islamic law are fundamentally different from any other system of law:

> A state may or may not claim that its law is, or accords with a particular religious law....It is also obvious that, while state law is usually territorially limited in scope, the population which observes a particular religious law is apt to be markedly transnational...[A]nalytically also the distinction between positive state law and customary law is problematic....Another difficulty in drawing a distinction between positive state law and customary law arises when we consider the ultimate basis of state law.[21]

For many obvious reasons Muslim religious scholars and jurists have been finding themselves at odds with legal systems that have developed in the nation state environment. In Gülen's discourse, realism has an important place. He takes the nation states as political and economic realities of our time. He believes that the major problems of many nation states could be addressed better if we all agree that ultimately the human being is a spiritual entity in the first place and that a spiritual approach to existing problems makes everybody's life easier and happier. To achieve this goal, the universal principles of Islamic law might help Muslims find a better and more practical approach to good governance and the rule of law.

Historically, the Companions of the Prophet apparently did establish a state for Arabs. However, that was a transitional stage before transforming the Arab state into an international polity previously unknown to the Arabs and the rest of the world. The idea of empire did exist, but the concept of the globalization of state power had yet to be born. Along with non-Arab Muslims, Arab Muslims had to spearhead the ideals of *ummah* that would create a super-national state as *dar al-Islam* (abode of peace) for all Muslims.

Neighboring nation states might find themselves at war, but neighboring Muslim states were supposed to live as brotherly nations on the basis of the teachings of the Qur'an and Sunna. However, in practical terms it was not always the case. Muslim nations did fight against each other for national supremacy or in territorial disputes. For the Sufis, state boundaries are not very meaningful or significant for individual Muslims and their spiritual salvation on earth and in the hereafter. A genuine Muslim is truly an internationalist in regard to states, whether they are friendly or hostile. Moreover, for a Sufi, no one should be regarded as his or her enemy merely for material or personal reasons. Furthermore, disagreement, even animosity, should not lead to any violent conflict with others and all kinds of war need to be stopped immediately. Such a Sufi stance is very difficult to explain or preach in a world where most of the great powers keep their system and economy on a war footing.

As Gülen asserts, "they [Sufis] reach the horizon of viewing all things and events differently with the consideration of Divine Oneness, and they are favored with being able to feel and interpret everything with the essential characteristics that the veil of corporeality hides. This can be regarded as the first step on the way of annihilation to the truth."[22]

Obviously, there has been more need of such saint-like Sufis in the midst of territorial disputes and ethnic conflicts. In history, for instance, after the fall of the Abbasid Caliphate in 1258, the Persian and Turkish armies fought each other for the control of Baghdad, which led to the destruction of harmony among Muslim nations. As a result of the instrumentalization of religion in politics, Persia turned from Sunni Islam to Shiite Islam, and thus the Iranian Muslims ultimately left the international mainstream of Muslim Sufi movements. Still Sufism as a movement remained alive in the major part of the Muslim world, especially on the Indian subcontinent, in Southeast Asia, and in the Maghrib (Northwest Africa). Despite the decline of Sufi movements in many parts of the world, prior to the European colonization of the Muslim world various *tariqa*s, whether progressive or conservative, dominated the socio-cultural life of the Muslim world.

Under the Ottomans, Sufis had no problems in communicating across borders and the Turkish Sufis came into contact with all kinds of *tariqa*s from other Muslim and non-Muslim countries. With a Muslim system in state power, it might seem that Muslims as a whole would not need Sufi movements. Gülen disagrees with this proposition. He thinks that there is always a need for "Sufi Masters" to keep the believers educated in the deeper meanings of the Qur'an and Sunna. "Adding to Qur'anic commentaries, narrations of Traditionists [who transmit and study Prophetic traditions] and deductions of legal scholars, Sufi masters developed their ways through asceticism, spirituality, and self-purification – in short, their practice and experience of religion."[23]

Since the industrial revolution, many Muslim countries have been suffering from an inferiority complex as they failed to use scientific discoveries and innovations in their nation building and other objectives. As a result, many Muslim regions of the world came under the direct and absolute domination of the European colonial powers. Muslims were also less innovative and competitive with their Western counterparts in productivity and distribution systems. Like their Western counterparts, many militant secularists in the Muslim world believe that Sufism and the Qur'anic teachings about vice and virtue have served as the main impediment to the economic and scientific progress and prosperity of the Muslim nations.

Gülen has often argued that a good knowledge of the different branches of science and technology is a very effective tool for the understanding of the Qur'an. Gülen is not committing any forbidden *bid'a* (innovation) here. He insists that without a balanced attitude toward life, science, our religious duties toward God, and our responsibilities toward those that surround us, no one can succeed in this life and the hereafter. The orthodox within any religious community may find Sufism unacceptable because of its openness and tolerant approach to all while some others say that Sufis put unnecessary emphasis on the mysteries of the spiritual life that can never be understood with full clarity. According to Gülen, the spiritual path contains various distinguishing subtle characteristics and particularities and demands continuous active participation of the people on this path for their spiritual journey or progression, which has essentially no limits with as many stages and ranks as there are believers, from Prophet Muhammad, the Pride of Humanity, to the most ordinary believer.

> Sufism, being a demanding path leading to knowledge of God, has no room for negligence or frivolity. It requires people on this path to strive continuously, like a honey bee flying from the hive to flowers and from flowers to the hive, to acquire this knowledge. The initiate should purify his or her heart of all other attachments; resist all carnal inclinations, desires, and appetites; and live in a manner reflecting the knowledge with which God has revived and illumined his or her heart, always ready to receive divine blessing and inspiration, as well as in strict observance of the Prophet Muhammad's example. Convinced that attachment and adherence to God is the greatest merit and honor, the initiate should renounce his or her own desires for the demands of God, the Truth.[24]

Journeying to any kind of perfection in religious matters and spiritual salvation cannot be achieved overnight; it is a life-long struggle for the total enrichment of the human character in every possible way at the individual and collective levels. Sacrifice for the cause of God ultimately brings visible and invisible benefits to the one who makes the sacrifice and his or her surroundings.

SUBMISSION TO GOD VIS-À-VIS THE EXALTED SOUL OF HUMAN BEINGS

To many people the idea of submission to God's commands seems nothing but a kind of spiritual or mental slavery that takes away freedom from individual life. They do not consider the fact that one can truly taste the great pleasure of salvation through servanthood to God and thus can be liberated from the slavery of endless cravings for worldly pleasures. The regulatory power of law seems to them to take away human freedom and liberty, whereas in reality it ensures the ample opportunity to enjoy freedom for all without harming each other. A Sufi tries to surrender to the "Will of God" without questioning apparent profit and loss and as a result, gets different types of benefits from heavenly sources. In fact, in Sufi understanding all human beings and creatures receive heavenly blessings without which their existence on earth would be impossible. Apart from this universal blessing from God on all human beings irrespective of loyalty toward any religion, ideology, or religious order, there are two general Qur'anic principles of reward and punishment based on deeds performed by a person. In Islam there is no belief in any form of collective punishment. Each human being will be rewarded or punished only for the merits and demerits of his or her own deeds. The following Qur'anic verses explicitly tell of this universal rule of reward and punishment for all human beings:

> Whatever (wrong) any human being commits rests upon himself alone; and no bearer of burdens shall be made to bear another's burden. (An'am 6:164)[25]

> And that man can have nothing but what he strives for. (Najm 53:39)

Here one can observe a striking difference between Islamic concepts of reward and punishment and the systems of reward and punishment in other theological discourses and legal doctrines. Islam does not only teach that every human soul will be rewarded and punished after the end of the individual's life on earth depending upon his or her deeds on earth. In Islamic theology, the issue of reward and punishment is much more complex. It is a continuous process of enrichment and turmoil in the human soul, and the mental and physical well being of any individual on earth. The

problem with many Muslims is that they divide or compartmental-
ize the blessings of God Almighty as if God does not care about the
reward and punishment of any person or nation on earth and He
will punish and reward for our deeds only after death.

This is a false perception of the Islamic doctrine of submission
to God's will on earth and its consequences. Any individual, Muslim
and non-Muslim alike, can get benefit or reward in this worldly life
or the hereafter by obeying God's rules on earth. Similarly, in the
hereafter one cannot avoid the disgrace one has earned by disobey-
ing God's commands to make a whole-hearted effort throughout
life to purify one's inner self and one's deeds. There are numerous
heavenly blessings on earth that are intended to be used by all irrespective of race, religion, or gender. However, misuse of any heavenly blessing leads to many bad consequences which are tanta-
mount to punishments from God. Of course, time plays a very important role in this process. So what we see or observe in front of
our eyes is not the end of the story. Unfolding events are here more
important than the present turmoil or pleasure one is experiencing.
This is indeed a very complicated spiritual exercise. While drawing
closer to God Almighty, one really cannot look down on others for
their failure to do so. On the other hand, a blessed person capable
of leading a pious life may be amazed to observe the mysteries that
surround us on daily basis. Gülen has explained this complex situation with the help of the Sufi concepts of *dahsha* (amazement) and
hayman (stupor).[26] Gülen very delicately contradicts those extreme
orthodox circles that believe that in Islam there is no scope for being so amazed by God's gifts on earth to the extent that one might
even lose control of oneself for a while:

> This can also be described as experiencing the truth that the
> Divine manifestations exceed the limits of reason, and that our
> love for Him goes beyond the limits of patience; amazement
> also means getting into a state beyond one's capacity of percep-
> tion.... So I feel that we should approach Moses' falling down
> in a swoon on Mount Sinai as his conscious amazement and
> shock, an attitude that he felt was fitting for him in the face of

God's partial manifestation of His Majesty in all Its transcendence and above all corporeality.[27]

LINK BETWEEN INNER QUALITIES AND GREAT ACHIEVEMENTS

With the decline of Muslim military power all over the world under colonialism and during the post-colonial era, the Muslim ruling elites have become bewildered into using their military force against their neighbors or against their own people. On the other hand, many Muslim religious scholars have indulged in merely rationalizing the Qur'anic verses with the help of literary meanings without knowing or even trying to understand the heavenly mysteries that surround us at every moment on earth. The many military defeats of Muslim armies by rival armies in the last two centuries have still not made clear to Muslim minds the essential point that those defeats were well deserved by Muslim nationalist forces or state armies. However, the military defeats of Muslim armies have had very little to do with the rise or fall of Islamic civilization.

The main catalysts of Muslim glory in upholding Islamic civilization are the people who are dedicated to achievement of a just system in every aspect of human life, including the judicial system. Gülen refers to such people as "physicians of the soul and reality whose hearts are open to all fields of all knowledge: perspicacity, culture, spiritual knowledge, inspirations and divine blessings, abundance and prosperity, enlightenment; from physics to metaphysics, from mathematics to ethics, from chemistry to spirituality, from astronomy to subjectivism, from fine arts to Sufism, from law to jurisprudence, from politics to special training of religious Sufi orders."[28] Thus, Gülen's understanding of Sufism is very broad. In this perspective, inner qualities are the key to the greatest achievements in this world and the hereafter.

Today too much emphasis on benefits for a tiny segment of the total population of a country or region ultimately renders the entire state or nation bankrupt. In the past, many nations and ethnic groups of humble means successfully contributed a great deal to the enrichment and emancipation of a particular religion or civilization while the destructive efforts of many modern states have already horrified all peace-loving people.

> Compared with previous centuries, people may well be wealthier and enjoy more convenience and comfort. However, they are trapped in greed, infatuation, addiction, need, and fantasy much more than ever before. The more they gratify their animal appetites, the more crazed they become to gratify those appetites.... And so they break with true human values a little more each day.[29]

To become a truly human being one needs to acquire good qualities in one's soul infused from heavenly sources and this is a never ending process of making oneself available for the well being of others, a process which must be pursued to its final fruition. The issues of justice are the founding stones for all parties that come into contact by agreement or by chance. The concept of justice in Islam is neither static nor so elastic that it can be used for evil or anti-people purposes.

Knowing well that Islam is a religion of justice, development, and emancipation for all, some Muslim circles seek to ensure the Islamic judicial system and spiritual salvation through the imposition of criminal justice on unwilling people in society. However, God made it very clear that according to Islamic principles no one should be compelled to become Muslim. Moreover, the criminal justice system is only a very tiny part (maybe one percent) of the overall social and state system. Thus the concept of surrender to the Will of God is quite broad and needs to be understood at different levels depending upon the concrete situation of the people and states concerned.

> In an Islamic society, the goal of every sub-system is to evolve an Islamic framework of life. If development means change—change towards a desired direction, then the goal of development in

> Islam is the movement away from non-Islam toward Islam. In
> the political realm as well as in the socio-economic sphere, the
> goal of Islam is to attain Islamic ideals. Likewise, in Islamic
> administration, the goal is to maximize Islamic values of human-
> ism of which *Adl* and *Ihsan* are important considerations.[30]

Individually human capabilities and exposure to the ever expanding universe and galaxies are very limited, but as a human race
our potentialities in many cases appear to be unlimited. However,
as a group engaging in productive work we need to prioritize our
activities for our own well being as well as for the welfare of others
and society at large. As a sub-group of workers or a professional
cadre we cannot engage in every area of specialization at the same
time. This is not a question of human freedom or dignity; this is an
issue all human beings have to deal with to make the best use of
their time, energy, and talent in the limited period of their adult-
hood and creative life.

The assumption that surrendering to the Will of God makes a
human being a slave of a religious elite or theological government
is completely wrong as the Islamic doctrines of *haram* (forbidden)
and *halal* (lawful) are rather a system of expanding human freedom
and liberty without harming others. This is a system designed to
resist anarchy at governmental as well as individual levels. However,
many religious scholars of our time have failed to preserve this delicate balance between unregulated and unrestricted human behavior on the one hand and the anarchic activities of a ruling military
elite on the other. Undermining the importance of *aql* (inherent
human sense of being human) many religious scholars simply fool
themselves into believing that the journey toward God with the
help of the Prophet's guidance is possible without using the talent
and wisdom with which human beings have been bestowed.
Gülen's perception of Sufism does not fail us here in navigating the
different ways and means of journeying toward God:

> In the language of Sufism, *yaqada* (wakefulness) means that an
> initiate must be aware, careful and sensitive with respect to

God's commandments at the beginning of the journey, and, without falling into any confusion, must be straightforward in thought, preserve spiritual balance, and act with insight in the face of the gifts that come as a result of advancing to the final point.[31]

The idea that Sufis are fatalists and lazy and do nothing but sit and remember God in words (*dhikr*) but without any action is simply a nonsense in Gülen's perception of Sufism. For Gülen, fatalism has no scope in Islam as such thinking makes "people [...] senseless objects."[32] However, Gülen does not defend all Sufis; he praises only those who try their level best to follow the genuine pathways prescribed by the Qur'an and Sunna. For Gülen, the Qur'an tells us many things and advises us in so many different ways that without full wakefulness, no one would be able to have a safe and successful journey toward God. Self-criticism may lead to some temporary uneasiness, and even unhappiness, but Gülen compares self-criticism to the light of wisdom in a believer's heart.[33] To keep that light working, a believer needs to be always vigilant against satanic forces or evil-doers that are always ready to inflict wounds on the hearts and minds of others or national and international interests, about which we are all concerned. Gülen notes the following on self-criticism:

> Self-criticism may be described as seeking and discovering one's inner and spiritual depth, and exerting the necessary spiritual and intellectual effort to acquire true human values and to develop the sentiments that encourage and nourish them. This is how one distinguishes between good and bad, beneficial and harmful, and how one maintains an upright heart.[34]

Many Westerners, non-believers, and secular-minded Muslims try to avoid the virtuous paths of Sufis, or for that matter any sensible Islamic way of life, simply because they would not be able to enjoy this worldly life or consume as much as they can. However, in the final analysis, a regulated and balanced way of life is always better than a vulgar and uncontrolled way of living. Gülen thinks that apparent suffering or discomfort in life from time to time is also beneficial for a strong believer who wishes to attain a higher degree or perfection in belief and in doing good deeds based on that convinced faith in the unity of God (*tawhid*):

> Sadness protects a believer's heart and feelings from rust and decay, and compels him or her to concentrate on the inner world and on how to make progress along the way. It helps the traveler on the path of perfection to attain the rank of a pure spiritual life that another traveler cannot attain even after several forty-day periods of repentance and austerity.[35]

Thus it is neither important nor possible for all Muslims or believers around the world to attain a similar type of strength in faith in *tawhid*, or even in the ways of obeying God and receiving the heavenly blessings spread throughout the known and unknown worlds. The most important thing in life is not to cause any harm to others, including all the creatures within our reach or beyond; and it is an imperative to do as much good as we can to ourselves and to others who come into contact with us directly or indirectly.

Sufism between *Inbisat* and *Itminan*

One of the main Western criticisms that Muslims face is that Muslims are very fearful of their God, while the Christian God is a very lovable God. Though there is not a different God for different religions and people—God is One and an integrated whole that has nothing to do with gender or number—followers of all religions try to portray their God different from the God of others to prove the supremacy of their God. As believers who know that they will be returned to God for judgment, Muslims call on God with both fear and longing in their hearts, follow Divine guidance, and put all their trust in God. They feel the expansion of the heart (*inbisat*) arising from hope. They know that if they follow Divine guidance, then they will have no fear in the end, by God's will. Accordingly, they try to do their best to live God-consciously, as if seeing Him (for even though we do not see God, He sees us at all times).

The real and ultimate God Almighty does not need any kind of evidence of supremacy as there are so many in-built proofs of His omnipotence and omnipresence in all things and phenomena that exists around us. The world of creatures is not composed of only those things that are visible to us. Islam gives many ideas of many invisible forces in and around the world and universe or in solar systems. In many different ways, the Qur'an articulates that everything on earth and in the heavens has been created for the benefit of humankind. The Qur'an also makes it very clear that no evil force can do any harm to any upright man or woman. Initially many readers of the Qur'an could not believe that humans have the capacity to multiply the many forces around them and make use of those forces for their own benefits and to create many means of destruction. Everything can multiply with or without the collaboration of forces and can multiply through its own progeny. By having their progeny on earth or by destroying their enemies on earth, everyone wishes to ensure their own longevity or happiness forever. God warns in the Qur'an that this is not the way to make oneself happy or great. Moreover, on the grounds of mere suspicion no one should be persecuted anywhere on earth.

> Behold, all who pledge their allegiance to thee pledge their allegiance to God: the hand of God is over their hands. Hence, he who breaks his oath, breaks it only to his own hurt: whereas he who remains true to what he has pledged unto God, on him will He bestow a reward supreme...But God's is the dominion over the heavens and the earth: He forgives whomever He wills, and imposes suffering on whomever He wills – and [withal,] He is indeed much forgiving, a dispenser of grace.[36]

God's grace and mercy is for all, but that does not mean that God will not punish people who are engaged in conspiracies and evil activities against innocent people or against entities designed to manifest heavenly blessings on earth. However, many wonder how same merciful God can be so "cruel" when it comes to punishing someone who has earned bad consequences through his or her evil activities. Is it a paradox in God's design for human beings to be imperfect or a limit on human ability to understand, reason, and appreciate fully the essence of human existence and its relation to God and to the universe?

Simple human reasoning has so many limitations that lead to many misunderstandings even in the material issues of life. Spiritual worlds are much more complicated to comprehend and to follow the natural directions hidden in God's words. God has delegated many powers to the system of natural forces and the human race in general, and nations and individuals in particular. God has warned people through Prophets of all kinds to pay attention to good people and resist the evil designs of wicked people. To make that principle clearer for the ordinary masses the Qur'an tells us many stories from the past. Almost all people, believers and non-believers alike, are aware that the Qur'an contains many stories very similar to those described in other, older religious scriptures.

The wisdom behind the stories contained in the religious scriptures is not easy to comprehend fully. One can easily manipulate the meaning of particular verses of any religious scripture and misuse them for one's selfish reasons or interests. Apart from some apparent contradictions, one can find many complicated expressions and rulings in religious scriptures. This might happen simply because of the limitation of a particular method of reasoning or understanding. No empirical method can be enough to comprehend fully what God has to say in the scriptures. Moreover, the preconceived ideas of a person or group of people might also lead to different interpretations of ideas derived directly or indirectly from religious scripture. This can be said about all the religious scriptures the human race has inherited. The Qur'an removes such dilemmas in the interpretation of its verses through examples set forth by God's Messenger. Now if people are very knowledgeable, sincere, and careful in finding the hidden and deeper meanings of the Qur'anic messages and the

Prophetic wisdom, they may be blessed with special knowledge and a nobler pattern of life. However, much of the time under the pressure of the political and economic situation, even scholars miss the underlying messages in the Qur'an in its entirety.

Gülen points out that simplistic human reasoning may quickly lead to confusion about the Qur'anic message and many readers may find contradictions in the linguistic expressions of the Holy Qur'an. However, a deeper study would reveal that the essence of holy messages is not confined within those linguistic expressions and apparent contradictions are merely indications of different consequences for different kinds of deeds and situations. The core principle that as Muslims or upright believers we need to stand up against the designs of known evil-doers remains the same. Regarding unknown wicked forces God has said again and again that heavenly forces will be enough to take care of the plotters of evil designs to destroy humanity and the sense of humility in communities and civil societies. To illustrate these points, the Qur'an refers to many events and stories known from other religious scriptures as well.

> We sent forth Moses with Our message: "Lead thy people out of the depths of darkness into the light, and remind them of days of God!"...Moses spoke unto his people: "Remember the blessings which God bestowed upon you when He saved you from Pharaoh's people who afflicted you with cruel sufferings...." If you are grateful, I shall most certainly give you more and more; but if you are ungrateful, verily, My chastisement will be severe indeed.[37]

Many Muslim scholars are not trained well enough to deal with the religious and ideological dichotomies that can be observed in many places in the Qur'an as well as this life. Some religious-minded authors do not understand the deeper meaning of God's justice with all its consequences leading to many blessings and cruel manifestations of the natural justice system. Gülen works hard and digs deep to understand for himself and his supporters how to keep their activities in line with God's blessed ideals and how to keep people away from the evil designs of satanic forces and wicked people's conspiracies to harm people and their environment. No arrogant and ignorant person could maintain such a path of wisdom and activism. Islam is not simply the name of some ideals or principles; it is the vision of a better and virtuous life for all, irrespective of race, religion, and gender. To find and to follow that path is an individual duty as well as a collective responsibility at the same time.

> Those who have realized their nothingness before God Almighty are balanced in both their religious lives and their relations with people....In many verses, the Qur'an relates that being a true believer depends upon one's integrity and truthfulness in words, actions, feelings, and innermost senses. It also regards such a degree of integrity and truthfulness as the basis of happiness in both this world and the next.[38]

Gülen stands firm in his conviction that it is very easy to preach religious teachings or values based on the apparent and hidden messages of the Qur'an, but very difficult to appreciate or follow them in the context of political reality and economic hardship. Here Gülen refers to a hadith: *No one, including me, can go to Paradise by his deeds unless God has enveloped me in His mercy.* In so many ways, Islam has proved that there is no sainthood that can be used as any kind of atonement to remove the consequences of sins, neither for an individual person nor a collective or nation engaged in deliberate sinful activities. However, the absence of such a doctrine of sainthood does not necessarily mean that Islam or Muslims underestimate the strength of the spiritual powers of extraordinary pious or virtuous people. A pious way of living is very distinct from the wicked life pattern that is very attractive and maybe materially rewarding for sinners.

The intellectual and spiritual struggle of Gülen and those inspired by him has nothing to do with a process of capturing the state or political power in Turkey or elsewhere. In the preaching and writing of Gülen, there is a very subtle, ground-breaking, intellectual war against the mischievous ways of holding and capturing public wealth by a few at the helm of political and military powers. He differentiates between the nature of absoluteness in God's Will and the in-built justice system maintained by heavenly or satanic forces on earth and in all the solar systems known or unknown to the human intellect and imagination.[39]

Unfortunately many Muslim governments continue to behave in very irresponsible ways and to mismanage or misuse the national wealth at their disposal and in turn make a huge number of people incapable of generating honest livelihood or just corrupt them. However, this has nothing to do with a poor understanding of the democratic system or rule of law by Muslims as many Westerners tend to believe. Many Muslim leaders and ruling elites do not care at all about their own people. One of the indicators of this phenomenon is the modern Muslim ruling elites and business communities' belief that much of the populace is an unnecessary economic burden on the nation because they are able to transfer public wealth to the West for their own personal and private benefit. As Yildirim notes,

> In contrast to what is observed in the rest of the world, in the Middle East, the idea of a renter state prevails thanks to the abundance of natural energy resources. The state, in the region, does not depend on its subjects for revenues, that is, taxes. The state, and to a large extent the ruling elite, collect the revenues from the sale of natural resources in world markets....The absence of dependence on society on the part of the state results in the absence of democratic accountability to the people.[40]

Turkish national statehood is an exception to this common Middle Eastern phenomenon of the almost complete isolation of the state mechanism from societal interests. As a result, despite all kinds of open and brutal assaults on the genuine religious feelings of the masses, the religious thinker Fethullah Gülen can call his people with good will and gestures to try to unite society with the state instead of bringing overly religious issues to the games of politics.

This essential component of Islamic wisdom is missing in contemporary Muslim movements in many parts of the world.

The relationship between the human soul and its Creator is a very delicate issue and without combining fear of God's disfavor with hope for eternal love and mercy from God at the same time and in the hearts and minds of the same people, no great cause on earth can be well served for a long period of time. Without strong *itminan* (complete happiness with God) at the individual level, one cannot reach a higher degree of *rida*, which means trying always to achieve the best in the worst situation and building a successful life without any kind of rebellion whatsoever. Gülen is a shining example of this who has neither revolted against his government nor his people but instead has achieved many religious and spiritual goals that many of his contemporaries among religious and political leaders have failed to appreciate fully.

CHAPTER 3

Gülen's Methodology of Schooling:
Educational Enlightenment
at Home and Abroad

GÜLEN'S METHODOLOGY OF SCHOOLING: EDUCATIONAL ENLIGHTENMENT AT HOME AND ABROAD

I t is a traditional belief that Islam does not allow a Muslim or institution to be non-political, especially if the person under consideration is an activist working for the betterment of the society in every way. This is one of the main reasons why most of the exponents of Islamic theories mostly support "political" Islam. Secularism as a state policy, on the other hand, is a relatively recent ideology that divides religious issues and mundane affairs in a distinct way so that state policies can be kept apart from religious issues. While secularists believe that this is the only way to keep state policies predictable in order to run a government smoothly, some Muslim scholars and philosophers find secularism very objectionable. They understand secularism as an anti-Islamic ideology, and they put their all efforts towards Islam as a political project to be implemented. They even claim that in the Qur'an and Sunna, more emphasis has been placed on politics and governance of state than any other issue. Gülen criticizes, however, both those who limit the Islamic law to a state system based on religious rules as well as hardline secularists who oppose the principles of Islamic law:

> Without looking at the meaning and implication of the word *Shari'ah* [Islamic law], they display an attitude opposing it. Whereas the word *Shari'ah* is, in a certain way, a synonym of religion, it indicates a religious life supported by God's commands, the Prophet's sayings and practices, and the consensus of the Muslim community. In such a religious life the principles that are related to the state administration are only 5%. The

remaining 95% is related to the articles of faith, the pillars of
Islam, and the moral principles of religion.[1]

The long-established thesis on Islamic state and governance are
shared by many sects in the Muslim world. Not many *ulama*
(Islamic scholars) have questioned the validity of such a political
stand, even after the demise of the Ottoman Caliphate,[2] which was
a unifying force in the Muslim world. The symbolic unity of all
Muslim nations under the Ottoman Caliphate and efforts to maintain purity in Islamic governance has remained as a precious cry in
many Muslim religious groups. The thoroughly secularized Turkish
government and people also could not ignore this inherent calling
of many million Muslims around the world. On the other hand, the
Turkish *ulama* under secularism have also transformed themselves
in their dress and behaviors so that they can no longer be compared
with the Arab or Iranian *ulama*. Under these circumstances Iranian
and Turkish *ulama* have taken their unique course to preserve the
sanctity of their religious beliefs and practice.

After World War II, both Iran and Turkey saw some liberalization of the strictly enforced secularization policies. As the Soviet
Union was no more so harsh in its atheistic policies both at home
and abroad, so neither Turkish nor Iranian governments could continue their overtly anti-Islamic policies toward their own people.
Because of Shiite interpretations of Islamic laws and preservation of
traditional *madrasa*s in Iran, Ayatollahs had always remained a con-
testing force against government whenever an issue related to Islam
was in question. The situation in Turkey was quite different. For a
long time, the *ulama* had lost its power to contest or compete with
the secular government in any way. However, the rivalry between
the two superpowers during 1960s made it difficult for the Turkish
government to combat popular Islam with only typical Western or
European secularism while the influence of the Soviet socialism and
atheism had started to grow among the Turkish youth as well.

Liberalization of secularism alone could not mitigate the
problem of hostility between the anti-Islamic forces and the forces

that had been trying to unite government and people with the religious emotions and feelings inherent in Muslim masses. Moreover, secular education has been failing to produce an honest and decent intellectual and working class to run a government in a Muslim country efficiently and effectively. Everywhere in the Muslim world, the corrupted and educated elite has become apparently aggressive and suppressive in implementing an agenda against the interests of the general population in order to please their foreign counterparts. In this regard, the minority hard-line secularist Turkish elite set themselves against the activities of religious people, perceiving them as backward and retrogressive while many from among the Turkish elite remain in a very unique position to tell its people that the ruling class is not hostile to any ideas and activities intended for public interest.

Under these circumstances since 1970s, numerous Gülen-inspired schools, educational centers, and universities have emerged to serve the educational needs of people both at home and abroad. Analyzing the Gülen-inspired educational institutions in Germany, Jill Irvine classified them into three categories: learning centers, intercultural centers, and private high schools.[3] All parents are interested in providing a good education for their children, while modern education in most cases makes children selfish, arrogant, and greedy. This is a common phenomenon we can observe in many countries. Muslims blame Western secular education for its valueless character, while religious education in the Muslim world has failed miserably to create human resources capable of running any modern business at state, regional, and international levels.

Gülen's ideal model of an education system is one that raises generations with both good ethics and all kinds of modern skills and capabilities. His idea of education focuses on combining good morality with science in education. The idea itself is not a completely new one. However, Gülen has freed this idea from all kinds of ideological bias. For Gülen, education is for seeking knowledge and developing good, moral character with competence in modern sciences in an effort to raise good human beings irrespective of race, religion, and ethnicity. How can this be achieved in the context of a particular country? And how can it be accomplished by depending upon a group of dedicated educators with no political affiliations, which are, indeed, detrimental to the students and of no benefit to the educational institution?

The main purpose of education should be free from all kinds of ideological affiliation. During 1960s and 1970s most Turkish parents were fearful of Marxist and atheistic influence on their children and thus found Gülen's educational ideas appealing. Many also feared religious indoctrination in Gülen's methodology of combining good morality with modern skills, but they ultimately found Gülen completely a modern man free from any extremist thoughts or ideas. The moral values about which Gülen is concerned are completely of universal character. "Gülen presents education as the only lasting solution for society's problems and the needs of humanity. Teachers who embody the universal values cherished by parents are the primary agents of civic activism."[4] Though such an idea in education is not new in the Muslim world, accomplishing this entirely in private sector was a completely new idea. Though Turkey was not a communist country, its education system was nationalized and was under absolute control of the government. Thus initially private schooling was not at all fashionable in Turkey. Moreover, value-based education has been looked down upon as a different name for religious education, which is strictly regulated in Turkey.[5]

The anti-Islamic Soviet constitutional legacy and practices resemble closely the Turkish policy of disestablishment of Islam through constitutional means. "Secularism was implemented through a series of decisive steps taken to disestablish Islam from its role in law and education, and as the official religion of the state."[6] With the help of the centralized State Directorate of Religious Affairs under the supervision of the government, the secular state has aimed at creating a "secular" *ulama*, who on its behalf offered all kinds of religious interpretations of Islam. Gülen was also supposed to be a "secular" *alim* to serve the official Islam upheld by the Turkish government. Because of his sermon in Bornova on *shariah al-fitrah* Gülen went through many difficulties. In the late decades of the Soviet era, it was not that dangerous in Turkey to explain Islam as *din al-fitrah*, if you did not touch on the political and economic aspects of Islam. Why, then, did Gülen get into trouble in explaining *shariah al-fitrah*?

One of the names of Islam is *din al-fitrah* (religion of human nature), and Gülen teaches *shariah al-fitrah* as the principles that are in effect in nature, or in brief, the laws of nature. In that specific Bornova sermon, Gülen discussed the two Divine Books, which are the Qur'an as the Revealed Book coming from the Divine Attribute of Speech and the Book of Universe, or Creation, as the manifestations of Divine Will and Power in the universe. By reading this Book of Universe, one can discern the Divine laws of nature such as physics, chemistry, biology, and math. Seeing these two books as the two sides of the truth, Gülen said that one can truly prosper in both worlds through abiding by both books. However, totally unaware of what this concept means, secret service people thought that Gülen was teaching *shariah* as a political doctrine. Obviously encouraged by the secret service, newspaper articles have appeared against Gülen, and he was put again under military surveillance for years, though prior to this event he was cleared from any suspicion after six months imprisonment without any crime committed.[7] Since the demise of the Ottoman State, even the word *shariah* has become sensitive in Turkey. However, the explanations given by Gülen about *shariah al-fitrah* knew no real controversy. He was urging Turkish Muslims to try to appreciate the deeper meaning of Islam and to rise above the controversy over state policies and/or less important issues related to Islam or Muslim sentiment. "Gülen's discourse is not only rhetoric; in praxis too he encourages all his followers to realize his ideals. After espousing Gülen as a spiritual and intellectual leader, his followers adapt themselves to his discourse and follow his *ijtihads*, even though he does not label them as *ijtihad*."[8]

Gülen was not talking about "political Islam" under the guise of *shariah al-fitrah*; his focus was rather on the natural sciences as a serious part of the school curricula. The combination of natural sciences with moral values by itself cannot ensure an educational system to flourish, however. The second step in Gülen-inspired schooling "is altruism, or the elimination of selfishness and establishment of a community service spirit in the field of education."[9]

The bad image that private schooling has received throughout the world for its profit-making character was a real problem that Gülen was concerned with. For Gülen, education is like food for the nurture of the soul and spirit in the upbringing of the next generation. Gülen-inspired schools have practically proven that Gülen had never aimed such schools to be established for profit making; he inspired hundreds of thousands of people from all walks of life, especially educators and business people, to establish schools of world class value and to educate students with full dedication so that students can overcome the utter selfishness and consumerism of modern life styles.

The underlying social dimension is the third aspect of Gülen-inspired schooling. For Gülen, schools cannot be taken as an isolated island of a society. Schooling needed to be performed in connection with societal affairs. All schools should bring together the educators, parents, and people with financial capability and will to spend material resources for the training and development of students in all aspects. Thus it is a tripartite agreement and cooperation between these three parties concerned.

The final point of Gülen-inspired schooling is related to the overall atmosphere of the education system. How can the most favorable environment be established for all, including the staff, students, parents, and sponsors of the schools and educational centers? There should be no tension between tradition and modernity or science and religion in the schooling system. This is a huge task to accomplish, especially in the Muslim countries where very quickly concerned parties in the education system find serious conflicting issues between science and religion or between tradition and modernity.

> While the roots of this educational movement lie in Anatolia, or modern Turkey, the world-wide popularity of the schools points to the fact that Gülen's educational paradigm has universal appeal. High achievement in math and sciences and emphasis on the exemplary moral character of teachers and its impact on the children's behavior are among qualities often praised by parents.[10]

No movement based on ethical and spiritual values can achieve such a goal of exemplary moral behavior for the teachers all the time, especially if they are involved in politics where conflicting parties or forces are contending for state power. To demonstrate an exemplary behavior or to become a role model for a large number of students is a difficult task to accomplish. This is also a life long journey for a devoted educator and professional teacher.

In terms of conceptual framework and theoretical postulate, Gülen's ideas and methodologies are not entirely new. For example, during the British colonial period a significant number of Indian Muslim scholars[11] advocated for this kind of education for the Muslims. However, many of them wanted to achieve their goals either under the British system or by boycotting it completely. The fundamental question was not how far we could stand with or without the British system. The main question was how we could incorporate moral values in modern education as well as character education in science education. We needed to have an education of our own funded by our own resources and supported by our own people.

Because of the rise of popularity of Gülen-inspired schools in Turkey, numerous business people and educators came forward to establish many private schools in Turkey. During 1960s, 70s, and 80s this unique educational system became a successful phenomenon in Turkey. During the 1980s, no secularist or nationalist group stood up against the Gülen-phenomenon of private schooling that had already become a success story and was popular among the Turkish younger generation irrespective of their religious or secular ideological affiliation. Then came the collapse of the Soviet Union.

Gülen Inspired Schooling after the Collapse of the Soviet Union

One may find thousands of stories of the process of the collapse of the USSR. However, the flawed educational system was the main reason for the collapse of the Soviet Union. From the outside, we see a sudden dismantlement of the USSR. As a person who studied in the USSR for graduate studies and research, I could see the Soviet Union was collapsing from within because of its meaningless educational system. The Soviet education was intended to create good human beings for the sake of communism, which was no longer competitive with Western capitalism during 1980s in terms of acquiring knowledge in science and technology, on the one hand, and in terms of creating good human resources that would be incorruptible and dedicated to the causes of humankind and human dignity, on the other hand. The Soviet atheism and officially endorsed Marxism had already become completely obsolete during the last decade of the Soviet era.

Conscious Turkish parents could also see this failing education system in the Soviet Union and could appreciate the value-based education system at so-called Gülen schools. Inspired by Gülen, thousands of people from all walks of life in pursuit of modern education with moral superiority and without any political affiliation took the opportunity to open Gülen-inspired schools in a number of former Soviet republics after the collapse of the USSR. The newly independent Muslim countries in Central Asia tried to find some hidden agenda of the Gülen-inspired schools in their territories. Even the KGB failed to find any such hidden agenda in Gülen-inspired schools, which were completely devoted to educational causes with a universal form of morality and human decency that every child needs most in his or her childhood. Except Uzbekistan, all other former Soviet states, including the Russian Federation, have allowed the Gülen schools to function in their territories.

> One of the most striking operationalizations of Gülen's fusion of commitment and tolerance is the nature of the Gülen movement, as it is often called, which has established hundreds of schools in many countries as a consequence of his belief in the importance of knowledge, and example in the building of a better world. The schools are a form of service to humanity designed to promote learning in a broader sense and to avoid explicit Islamic propaganda....A comprehensive survey of the Gülen movement goes far beyond the boundaries of this exploration but it is helpful to note that the schools are only one aspect of a vast and somewhat amorphous movement that involves anywhere between 200,000 and 4 million people worldwide and has a wide range of organization. Gülen's followers have created a Journalists and Writers Foundation that brings Islamist and secularist intellectuals together as well as symposia that promote interfaith dialogue.[12]

Those inspired by Gülen's ideas and the political activists for a revival of Islamic state or caliphate are very different in their views. Gülen is for spiritual and genuine intellectual revival of the Muslim nations for the betterment of the entire humankind. Muslim activists working for political power of any Muslim state have little time to devote to the causes pursued by Gülen, who does not indulge in any religious or ideological conflicts with any groups. However, he also distances himself from all kinds of state religiosity and does not hesitate to criticize certain examples of official Islam: "Supposedly there are Islamic regimes in Iran and Saudi Arabia, but they are state-determined and limited to sectarian approval."[13] Here, one may take Gülen as just a critic of Saudi or Iranian official Islam based on Hanbalism in its Wahhabi form and Shiism of the Jafari School respectively. Gülen does not like to see his Islamic vision blended with any sectarianism, which has already cost Muslim nations many things, including the caliphate and a world-vision of Islamic spirituality. Gülen and his schools are not at all for propagating any old or new sect within the *dar al-Islam* [land of Islam]. For Gülen, the entire humankind is within the House of Peace of God, and Muslims need to safeguard that peace at any cost. This is a peaceful Sufi way of Islam in practice and without a political ideology:

> Islam is a religion. It can't be called anything else. When the West defeated the Islamic world in military and technology, salvation was sought in politicizing Islam or transforming it into a political system. This resembles a modern version of Khawarij, whereas Islam as a religion is based on delighting the mind and brightening the heart. Thus faith and worship come first. The fruit of faith and worship is morality.[14]

When it comes to the issue of politicizing Islam, even a moderate Muslim would tell you not to over-politicize Islamic tenets, while Gülen tells us not to politicize Islam at all. Gülen is very firm in his attack on the theories of political Islam, which he believes is totally uncalled for. How is it then that Islam as a complete code of life is accepted by all sects within Islam? No one in the Muslim community would quarrel with you about the *Din al-Islam* [religion of Islam] which strongly and categorically refers to the idea of the complete code of Islam. Referring to *din al-fitrah* as *sharia al-fitrah*, Gülen tells his audience that both the rise and fall of any system would ultimately depend on the secret will of God-Almighty upon which no one can claim authority or superiority.

Many Islamic tenets have never been as highly politicized as we have witnessed during the colonial period, which cast a huge ongoing shadow on all Muslim nations irrespective of their national, ethnic, and sectarian identities. Many in the West cannot believe or appreciate that because of the colonial exploitation of Muslim masses, Muslim leaders in any country have been able to connect the Crusade[15] era with the modern colonialism that has engulfed almost the entire Muslim world.

We are talking with you about the negatively counter and destructive role of colonialism. Now we need also to add internal factors to this that are related to some representatives of the society, who are at a loss in the material process of imperialism. These representatives of our countries are at a loss when the imperialist countries with the help of scientific and industrial progress or just by colonization and grabbing resources of the peoples of Asia and Africa accumulated wealth in the West. Our representatives thought that industrial development has automatically nullified our convictions and cannons. For example, as they have reached the moon, then you need to put aside your own laws. What relation is there between Islamic law and reaching the moon?! Why don't they see that countries with conflicting social systems have been competing with each other in scientific and industrial progress and battling over the cosmos? Even if they reach Mars or fly through the entire galaxy, they would not achieve moral quality and spiritual depth, and they would not be able to solve their own social problems or be happy in addressing social problems or removing obstacles in restoring religious and moral principles. ....Colonizers wish to convince us that Islam has nothing to do with power and its organs. Even if there are some laws in Islam, there is no one to follow those laws and in general, Islam is nothing more than a legislator. It is clear that colonial propaganda is a part of the plan to take away Muslims from the politics and the fundamentals of governance. Such a plan is totally against our basic religious conviction.[16]

One would wonder how Gülen had to overcome such serious political tones in regard to Islamic thought, on the one hand, and anti-Islamic propaganda of the West on the other hand. Many supporters of Gülen and Muslims in general do subscribe the idea that after the fall of the Baghdad-based caliphate, the *ulama* practically froze the institute of *ijtihad* as a method of updating Islamic thoughts to make it easier for people to follow or to make it tangible to comprehend Islam-related issues fully. It appears that Gülen has very little interest in the discourse of revealing who did what in regard to controversial issues related to Islam, especially when it comes to a specific practice for acquiring knowledge for the enlightenment of soul and deeds. For Gülen, there are not too many fundamental issues over which Muslims need to quarrel, rather a Muslim needs to devote himself or herself to acquiring knowledge and to good works as much as one can do.

Depending upon one's personal situation and ability, one can make an Islamic and/or Muslim practice so fundamental in his or her religiosity that it is sometimes useless to argue about it with a concerned person or authority in charge. Also, in Islam the domain of certain issues might be bigger or smaller depending upon the harshness and easiness of the situation and the capabilities and attitude of the concerned parties and people therein.

> The headscarf isn't one of Islam's main principles or conditions. It's against the spirit of Islam to regard uncovered women as outside of religion. We have so many things in common. First, we must try to come together on the pillars of faith and principles or main commandments of worship. Then we can discuss other matters. Where the main pillars of Islam are attacked by its enemies and not observed by its followers as they must be, we cannot divide on matters of secondary importance.[17]

We should make it clear first that while Gülen urges Muslims not to split among themselves, he does not even imply Muslim women to take off their headscarves. Here, considering the issues of the fundamentals of the religion of Islam (*usul*) and the ancillary branches of the religion (*furu'*), he reminds people of the fact that Muslim women who do not wear headscarf are not outside of the religion as the current issue of the wearing of headscarf for the Muslim women is a secondary matter (*furu'*) in relation to the fundamentals of faith Islam. At least theoretically speaking, reminding people of this principle of the Islamic law was supposed to be an easy matter according to the rules and regulations laid down in the Qur'an and Sunna. However, from a historical, political, and social perspective, no famous religious leader prior to Gülen could come up with such clear-cut and distinct voice in favor of female students who are not allowed to wear headscarves in schools. Here we find

Gülen a revolutionary thinker, pushing the envelope far enough to achieve the core objective of educating all human beings at any cost. In fact, this *hijab* issue interpreted by the conservative Indian *ulama* kept the entire Muslim women folk illiterate in the entire Indian sub-continent and that contributed negatively to the sociopolitical and economic development in this region.[18]

Colonial powers dominating and exploiting the Muslim world have already talked a lot about education for women and empowering Muslim women in the Muslim countries. However, their policies are insignificant or counter-productive in terms of time and resources they used for it, while by measurement of any yardstick the achievement of Gülen-inspired schools both in and outside of Turkey is remarkable by all accounts. Despite the disadvantageous position and unfavorable situation in many former socialist countries and Third World countries, Turkish schools inspired by Gülen's altruism have achieved commendable goals in disseminating knowledge in natural and social science education.

In the West, very often you hear that the *madrasa*s (religious schools) are the main breeding ground for fundamentalists, who are very eager to kill Westerners, especially Jews and Christians. As if by killing some non-Muslims, the so-called Islamic fundamentalists would be able to destroy the entire Western civilization and replace it by an Islamic civilization. In the final analysis, this is the essence of the theories of the clash of civilizations, articulated and propagated by the Western media and anti-Islamic media of the Muslim World.[19]

The very concept of modern *madrasa* education is an "invention" of the European colonizers, who had practically ruled the entire Muslim world for a long time. Neither the division of knowledge as sacred and secular nor education based on merely or purely some religious texts and their interpretations given by some authors in absolute isolation with other branches of knowledge and social sciences such as economy is permissible within the Islamic worldview. Social and economic reforms are the foundation of political affairs of any government. Thus Muslim rulers had never dared to divide education along the lines of economic and non-economic principles and values. After capturing the Muslim countries one after another, the colonizers separated education in terms of religion and secularism. Such a dividing line in acquiring knowledge has proved to be disastrous for the socioeconomic development of the Muslim world.[20]

Gülen has accepted the constitutional principles of secularism and nationalism of the country as a reality and believed that education is the right place where Turkish Muslims irrespective of their party affiliation can contribute to create a "golden generation" who would be dedicated to national and global causes. The preamble of the Turkish constitution reads:

> The recognition that no protection shall be afforded to thoughts or opinions contrary to Turkish national interests, the principle of the indivisibility of the existence of Turkey with its State and territory, Turkish historical and moral values or the nationalism, principles, reforms and modernism of Ataturk and that, as required by the principle of secularism, there shall be no interference whatsoever of the sacred religious feelings in State affairs and politics.

Under such a constitutional system, one would wonder how Gülen has kept his faith-inspired works going. Gülen did not enter into any controversy with the constitutionally declared ideological populates under secularism, nationalism or Kemalism, rather he put all the emphasis on spiritualism and educational enlightenment to overcome all problems. As an Islamic scholar in secular Turkey, Gülen is a remarkable success story for all quarters concerned who are interested in making the Turkish nation a dynamic and independent power in the world. One of the fundamental needs of any society or state is to nurture human souls, which would ultimately safeguard the interests of state, nation, and humanity. To achieve this vital goal, schooling and the educational system need to be designed to cultivate good qualities in the hearts and minds of the people from the very beginning of their life so that bad inclination in human instinct may subside and so that space for good spirit can be broadened for the benefits of others as well.

To achieve this major objective for the entire society, many nations, ideologies, and religions have adopted numerous doctrines to be materialized in schooling and preparing better human resources. Moreover, it is important to make sure that the qualities acquired at school during childhood and youth can be properly used at latter stages in life, especially during their professional career. Thinkers like Plato, Karl Marx, and many others have wished to deprive the ruling elites from all kinds of ownership and exclusive private life so that rulers could not use state power, wealth, and personal relationships for their own benefit only. Such an idea cannot be supported or endorsed by any major Islamic tenets. However, the misuse of property rights and abuse of family and/or blood relations has reached to very dangerous levels in many countries. As a result, it has increasingly become difficult for common people to take advantage from any existing legal system or rule of law.

Under these circumstances, Gülen works for the betterment of society without clashing with any existing system, taking into consideration the realities of the context and situation. Thus by taking cognizance of the existing legal and political order on one hand, Gülen expresses his vision of change for the whole of society. On the other hand, he expresses this vision in a way that any objective mind finds Gülen's criticism of his own society constructive.

> Especially today, as life has become more intricate and complicated, as the world has globalized, and every problem has become an all-encompassing, planetary problem, it is vital that those competent in natural science, engineering, and technology, which are most of the time considered to be good and proper by Muslims, should participate alongside those men of high caliber who know Islamic essence, reality, spirit and sciences. ...According to different circumstances and eras, the conduct and the composition of the consultative committee might change, but the qualifications and the attributes of those

select people, such as people from knowledge, justice, social education and experience, wisdom and sagacity, must never change. Justice means fulfilling all compulsory duties, but avoiding all that are forbidden and nothing contrary to human values should be done; knowledge comprises religious, administrative, political, and scientific expertise.[21]

Most exponents of Islamic doctrines of our time either misunderstand or underestimate the impact and influence of the globalization process in the Muslim world. Moreover, not many Muslim countries could make use of advanced science and technology to reap the benefits of globalization and thus suffer from serious negative consequences of globalization. Muslims would do better if they could take such phenomenon as their own failure as well. What Muslims need to do today is to fix their internal problems as quickly as possible by their own initiative and feel it a necessity to contribute to global systems in all positive ways in order to make our planet a better place to live and to engage in creative activities. Jill Carroll's analysis is noteworthy here:

> For Gülen, there is no other way to structure society that deserves to be called "human" and certainly no other way that can be called "Islamic." Human beings have within them the capacities to achieve perfection as humans, and those who internalize and actualize that perfection in themselves must influence society, as rulers or consultants, or grassroots community leaders. For any of these things to happen, people must be educated in an intentional, proper way. The schools of the transnational Gülen movement are contemporary initiatives in this endeavor, and they seek to educate their youth from all sectors of society to become highly trained and virtuous people who, like Confucian superior men, influence everything and everyone around them with the force (*te*) of their knowledge, goodness, and beauty.[22]

Here comes to mind a fundamental question as to what makes a man humanist. Can a fatalist or determinist be a humanist? Fatalism and determinism have apparently very little to do with Islamism as an ideology or world-view. However, many dogmatic interpretations of numerous Qur'anic verses produced by many Muslim and non-Muslim scholars alike give an impression that Islam stands for a strong fatalistic way of living. Moreover, backwardness of Muslim nations in modern science and technology and reflection of that backwardness in real material life have led to an overwhelming inferiority complexity in the hearts and minds of many millions of Muslims.

Furthermore, unlike the majority of people in the West, Muslims still tend to believe that big players are there to undermine the rights of the poor and ordinary masses. In many Muslim countries half of the population lives below poverty line, which has been maintained for several centuries now for the benefits of the affluent class of the West as well as Third World and Muslim countries.

Gülen is very cautious in presenting such a global dilemma of mitigating economic, social, and cultural conflicts of interests between the nations. His intention is not to blame anyone in any wholesale way for the miseries of Muslim people. Gülen tries to present the problems objectively, seeking local and international remedies to those problems without instigating hatred to anybody or other religions.

> [O]ur truth is tightly related to the spirit of the infinite....We feel that we have been on the way to such a luminous world for years. We deal neither with searching for the signs and symptoms of the awaited dawn nor with investigating magical numbers and dates for mysterious future happenings. By evaluating everything that the needle of the compass of our souls shows under the guidance and leadership of Divine realities, we will try to relate and connect ourselves to the Divine Will by means of our own willpower; we will become like those heroic people who spent everything they had on this way; we will use, spend, and sacrifice from our own lives and wealth; we will keep on walking on this way until we meet the Divine Will and what it presents and promises.[23]

Such a divinity was not unknown to the West as well. However, unfortunately the Western mindset has been working against such spirituality of selflessness for quite some time, and the consequence of that indifferent attitude to others is now very obvious around the world. We cannot blame the West or neo-colonizers endlessly for our own miseries. We are also to be blamed for many miseries we have created for our own nations and people. For example, Turkey is a very resourceful country and there should be no reason why the Turkish economy should be controlled by outsiders or by a tiny corrupted elite of its own.[24] Compared to many Muslim countries, Turkey is not that corrupted, but its military expenditure as a member of NATO and human rights records has been questioned by many quarters. NATO has lost much of its military significance, and the EU has acquired different kinds of significance for the Turkish economy, politics, and human resource development. It is unlikely that Turkey will be accepted as a full member of EU soon, and as a member of NATO, it will remain under different kinds of scrutiny from friends and foes alike.

> We must rely on ourselves and our own powers, regardless of whether we believe they come to us from God, as Gülen does, or not, like Sartre, and refuse to expect something or someone outside of us to do our work for us. To push our responsibility onto others is to live in "bad faith," to use Sartre's phrase which, interestingly, squares quite well with Gülen's assessment of people of faith who refuse responsibility—they live a "bad faith.[25]

Gülen believes that a vast majority of problems we face in our individual and collective life is due to our egoistic attitude toward life, and value-based education may cure many of the problems we have been facing in our mundane affairs.

Value-based education does not need any special kind of indoctrination to any particular ideology or political system, which might be incomplete, inadequate, and out of date. Indoctrination to socialist, capitalist, or religious cults might be dangerous for an individual life, society, and even for a state. Islam does not allow any kind of indoctrination as such and permits Muslims to choose to follow any of the particular school of jurisprudence. Too rigid a way or thought in addressing mundane problems may lead to create unnecessary hardship for others, which is the anti-thesis of the basic Qur'anic idea that God Almighty does not make human life unbearably difficult for anyone. It appears that Gülen's success of moral and educational enlightenment for the people he inspired has become a reality because of the implementation of this golden rule derived from the essence of the *din al-fitrah*. As Gülen puts it:

> Islam also is seen as a political ideology, for it was the greatest dynamic in the Muslims' wars of independence. Thus it has become identified as an ideology of independence. Ideology tends to separate, while religion means enlightenment of the mind together with belief, contentment, and tranquility of the heart, sensitivity in conscience, and perception through real experience. By its very nature, religion penetrates such essential virtues as faith, love, mercy, and compassion. Reducing religion to a harsh political ideology and a mass ideology of independence has erected walls between Islam and the West, and has caused Islam to be misunderstood.[26]

Many Islamic principles lead to diverse political interpretations, but this cannot reduce Islam to merely a political ideology. The primary concern of the Islamic belief system and action plans based on this are to make human beings spiritually-oriented and dedicated to the causes of humanity, peace, and glorifying God.

CHAPTER 4

Gülen's Approach to the
Qur'an and Ideal Society

GÜLEN'S APPROACH TO THE
QUR'AN AND IDEAL SOCIETY

It can be argued that it should not be a difficult task to read and truly comprehend the Qur'an in Arabic, if one knows the language, or its interpretation in any other language. It is true that any individual who knows the language of the Qur'an can grasp something from it; however, even an Arab might truly be ignorant or confused about the real messages of the Qur'an, despite the fact that he or she can read Arabic. This is a dilemma for any serious reader of the Qur'an who would like to benefit from the Qur'anic lessons as a whole rather than indulging in any particular word, term, or verse about a particular story, theme, or different aspect of prophetic missions. Without being well-versed in the entire text of the Qur'an, it is sometimes even dangerous to come to a conclusion about the spirit and apparent meanings of particular verses, especially if you would like to take them as legal injunctions or mandatory religious duty.

In line with the Divine incentive to study and reflect upon the Word of God, Islamic scholars are encouraged to discover the hidden beauties of the Qur'an as there is always more to be found in the verses of the Qur'an. Finding or discovering a new interpretation of any Qur'anic verse might not be a difficult task for experts of exposition and commentary who have linguistic competence and the knowledge of the prophetic traditions and who expend great effort in the reflection of verses and pay great attention to the disciplines and methodology of exposition. It is also to be noted that since all the interpretations of the Qur'an are but partial representations that favor certain meanings over others, undermining and discrediting all other interpretations with a new one cannot be a good strategy for any knowledgeable person and pious man.

> Those who cannot see the Qur'an with their own inner depth and those who do not accept the person of the Prophet as the most skillful navigator of the depths of the Qur'an are unfortunates who have drowned in their own depths–if indeed we can call this a depth... In fact, the Qur'an is a source which has an enigma so deep and a purity so vast, a source with such richness that all those who address it can see that it is beyond the horizon of the sphere of their understanding, and they can experience the security of having such a source. Then with the discovery of their own horizon of understanding, they watch like a rainbow, a triumphal arch that is always just beyond the point that the follower has reached. Piety is such a transcending interpretation of the source of light that pours into life through a chrysolite prism, molding and shaping it, that those who feel it witness an inimitable "ease of flawless expression," even though they can see their level of understanding always expressed in the Qur'an.[1]

Here, Gülen expresses the notion that everyone can understand the Divine Word to the depth of the horizon of his or her perception, thus pointing out the danger that some people may even claim that everything in the Qur'an is crystal clear for them, and, therefore, its literary meaning is not so difficult to comprehend. However, any specialist of the Arabic language would find many different meanings of the same word or verse used in the Qur'an. For example, the first revealed word "Read!" in the Qur'an could refer to many things from "reciting" to "discovering," from "contemplating" to "meditating." Every single word used in the Qur'an has so many potential meanings, and an interpreter of the Qur'an, therefore, prefers one meaning over others in their work. Gülen stresses that the Qur'an as the "Word of God" revealed to the Prophet can be interpreted to the extent that a Divine word can be interpreted by human perception. Any interpretation of the Qur'an only has value in proportion to the interpreter's learning, knowledge, horizon of perception, and skills.

Early Muslim generations were very successful in interpreting and conveying the universal messages of Islam and in reforming many nations and peoples who came in touch with the early civilization of Islam. Gülen argues a constant reconsideration of the Qur'an, likening it to a rose that continues to bloom, revealing new petals for interpretation and analysis. He emphasizes that we are all children of our own time and that time and conditions are important means in interpreting the Qur'an. As time goes on the Divine Message becomes younger, and more of its hidden beauties are explored. After fourteen hundred years of its revelation, various aspects of the messages of many Qur'anic verses unfold themselves now in new and different ways for different people depending upon one's capability to understand or the circumstances one has to deal in real material life.

One should not undermine or discredit all other interpretations by a new one. Yet, it is possible to see some interpretations as a critique of other interpretations. For example, a Muslim feminist may think that she has every right to read and interpret the Qur'anic verses in feminist perspective as she believes that most of the Qur'anic interpretations have been made on the assumption that man is superior to woman. Others offer yet other interpretations, like that of Asma Barlas, stressing that the Qur'an put all men and women on equal terms in the eyes of God:

> Breaking with another feminist tradition, I also do not read the Qur'an as a dual-gendered text, that is, a text that has both male and female voices in it. For Muslims, the Qur'an is God's Speech and not the work of human authors... [W]hen I refer to the Qur'an's egalitarian "voice," I am not referring to tendencies in the Qur'an that have been submerged or lost because of the patriarchal nature of its exegesis and the gendered nature of human language.[2]

How far we can claim that some Qur'anic verses have patriarchal or matriarchal tone, when these verses are meant for all people and for all times? Indeed, one should not be surprised to see, among a great number of studies and resources about the Qur'an, the works of many Muslim and non-Muslim interpreters of the Qur'an, in whose interpretations certain issues take precedence over all other issues, aside from those works of the Orientalists who select only certain verses that fit their message, citing them exclusively for their own purposes. Thus all individuals with their particular worldview, religious motivation, or political objective may find their own explanation and reflections of their thoughts in the Qur'anic verses.

Gülen from his early life as a preacher, author, and mentor of cross-sections of people have tried to avoid any kind of sectarian or partisan type of interpretations and understanding of the Qur'an. He draws attention to the unifying feature of the Qur'an—the common point of reference for all Muslims—which often surprises Western scholars:

> In contrast, Christianity's Gospels have not survived in their original language; the language of the earliest surviving version of these Scriptures is a dead language. ...For almost 200 years, Western scholars have subjected the Qur'an to the same rigorous scrutiny. However, they have failed to prove that it was subjected to a similar process. They discovered that Muslims, like Christians, sometimes split into disputing factions. But unlike Christians, all Muslim factions sought to justify their position by referring to the same Qur'an.[3]

In the fourteen centuries of Islam, many jurists have inferred laws from the Qur'an and based their juridical reasoning on it, and many interpreters have derived different meanings from it.

Along with numerous people who have supported their point of view with Qur'anic truths, it is also possible to see in the long history of Islam the conflicting parties amongst Muslims trying to justify their own personal view point by using deductively every reference in the Qur'an to prove and legitimize their stance against others. This very antiquated practice is detrimental to the major objective of Islam to bring all kinds of Muslims under a broader umbrella of universal peace and tranquility for the benefit of the entire humankind.

THE VALUE OF REASON AND THOUGHT

One of the major problems Muslims have faced for centuries is the freezing of interpretations of the Qur'anic messages, correlating them only with the huge number of *hadith* compilations selected and arranged according to topics based on different ideals conceived by different Muslim scholars. Of course, this is not to say that the scholars now should be content with interpreting the Qur'an using solely their own reason without referring to the Prophetic Traditions since the first and foremost interpreter of the Qur'an was the Prophet, peace and blessings be upon him. The interpreters of the Qur'an should know how the Prophet interpreted a verse while making expositions of the related verse, especially if the Prophet already interpreted that verse in a plain way that does not allow a variety of interpretations. Whether the Prophet interpreted all of the Qur'an is another issue to consider. Most of the scholars agree that the Prophet interpreted the Qur'an as much as was necessary. In doing so, the Prophet has kept the door open for making expositions and commentaries until the Last Day, and people are encouraged to use their reason and intellect to find new insights and make fresh interpretations on the Qur'an. This notion is contrary to the claims of some Muslims who think that the door of *ijtihad* (independent reasoning) was closed, a notion that has caused a stagnation of reasoning as well as the criticism of some Orientalists or people with bias:

> It is possible, again, to see both divine inspiration and particular social circumstance in development of the tradition. [A]ristotelian logic was known and severely criticized as incompatible with koranic learning. So, as the organization of the Koran itself is chaotic, so the structure of islamic [sic] law cannot be made systematic, in any western sense. The intellectual tools are

not available, or at least not authorized by the leading statement of the tradition.[4]

Indeed, the Qur'an invites reason to confirm all its pronouncements, and the Divine Messages are better understood in a world where reason, knowledge, and science prevail. The critics of Islam are either moved more by their anti-Islam bias than genuine concern and interest or are ignorant of the disciplines of the methodology of the exposition of the Qur'an. The experts of the Qur'an exert great exegetical efforts in their approach to many issues from different, wider perspectives without diverting from the rules of the Qur'anic exposition methodology which is indeed well-established. The methodology of Qur'anic exposition does not reject any important source of human knowledge if it has not been proven to be destructive to human beings and nature. Indeed, the interpreters of the Qur'an are encouraged to be conversant not only in religious sciences, but also other sciences, for example, sociology, history, and psychology, as this knowledge is necessary in Qur'anic expositions and commentaries. Moreover, a good-hearted and knowledgeable Muslim is supposed to learn how and when to accept or reject Aristotelian or any other theory when that is helpful or irrelevant to solve a problem. Aristotle, for instance, did support slavery as a system to make the economy functional just as many Americans did until recent times. Even the so-called monumental document of human freedom and liberty, the Magna Carta, could not conceive in any form to treat slaves equally in regard to their livelihood and considered slaves as any other commodities in the market place to be sold and bought at any time according to the wish of the slave-owners. Many biased people in the West do not ask a simple question: why have no Western legal documents or constitutions, from the Magna Carta to very recent times, considered that slaves were good human beings as they are today. Any typical Western criticism of the Qur'an is full of unfair attacks against the Islamic principles that were either misunderstood or misinterpreted without giving any appropriate consideration to the time, place, and circumstances of the revelation.

What the critics of Islamic law do not appreciate is the fact that the Qur'an for the first time in human history considered all individuals, especially slaves and women, who had unfortunately been seen inferior in society, as full human beings with similar heavenly souls that any man, rich or poor, can be endowed with by the grace of God. The practical treatment of the slaves and women in terms of their right to life, work, livelihood, and worship under the rule of Prophet in the city state of Medina clearly demonstrated that the Prophet of Islam had aimed to put an absolute ban on all kinds of slavery, but he did this gradually and not by using coercive methods against slave-masters. The Prophetic idea was that one who is a true servant of God is not a servant of others as all creation are the slaves of the Almighty God, and no slave-owner had any right to look down on slaves or mistreat treat them in any way. As Gülen puts it clearly, the Prophet had demonstrated what a comprehensive system he had adopted to free practically all slaves at any cost:

> Islam established, as a first step, strict principles on how to treat slaves, as seen in the following *hadith*s: "Those who kill their slaves will be killed. Those who imprison and starve their slaves will be imprisoned and starved. Those who castrate their slaves will be castrated,"[5] and "Arabs are not superior to non-Arabs; non-Arabs are not superior to Arabs. White people are not superior to black people; black people are not superior to white people. Superiority is only in righteousness and fear of God."[6]
>
> As its second step, Islam enabled slaves to realize their human consciousness and identity. It educated them in Islamic values, and implanted in them a love of freedom. On the day of their emancipation, they were fully equipped to be useful members of the community as farmers, artisans, teachers, scholars, commanders, governors, ministers, and even prime ministers.[7]

This Islamic stance was one of the reasons why the number of former slaves among early Muslims was huge in almost all societies that accepted Islam. It is intellectually difficult and spiritually inconceivable for a western materialist or secular minded Muslim to comprehend the *hikma* (wisdom) of the Prophet Muhammad, peace and blessings be upon him, in his gradual addressing of the controversial issues of the time. This Islamic stance against slavery and its emphasis on equality, regardless of race, gender, or background, is just one example towards establishing an ideal society.

Ground-breaking advancements, especially in science and technology that afforded the West tremendous opportunities of prosperity, are positive aspects of modern civilization. On the other hand, this civilization aims at nothing except out of self-interest to the point that it has become quite destructive to social and family life as well as everything that surrounds us in nature. Their material gains and market dominance has been at the expense of developing countries. This is indeed the case with many nations or peoples who got the chance to dominate other nations in history. In many cases, Muslim rulers also could be accused of harming others and violating the rights of others. However, the destructive power of the leaders in developed countries today has no parallel in the entire human history. With the powerful technological know-how, certain western elements with diabolical plots now can penetrate into any corner of the world and conduct destructive activities. Unfortunately, anti-democratic groups that antagonistically work behind the scenes in Turkey were about to be a part of this whole-scale destructive methodology of dictating others in their internal affairs.

Since the rise of ultra-nationalist and extreme secularist forces, the modern Turkish state has always tried to become an integral part of Europe or the West. With such a dilemma as a nation-state, Turkey did not know to what its soul should be attached. Many practicing Muslims did not know that calling for an Islam limited within the boundaries of a state as an idea in itself is the anti-thesis of Islamic unity and brotherhood.

Encouraging people to serve for humanity in different parts of the world, Gülen has never called for any Islamic state or Islamic revolution in Turkey or elsewhere. He put forth clearly why the

Turkish journey to Islamic revival could not be the same as it was in Iran after the Islamic revolution. Yet, anti-democratic elements inside the state went after Gülen, attempting to isolate him from his enthusiasts and to intimidate him continuously and severely to stop him preaching his peaceful messages based on the Qur'an.

It might be true that some Muslims cannot grasp fully the depth of the peaceful mission of Islam and the Qur'an on earth and may indulge in destructive methods to take revenge against colonialists, imperialists, or the evil forces that had practically destroyed the Muslim world in many ways. As a result, some people keep saying that they need to hold the Western powers accountable legally and morally for the destruction they did to the Muslim nations. However, western scholars take the issue other way around. Bernard Lewis, for example, argues:

> To a western observer, schooled in the theory and practice of western freedom, it is precisely the lack of freedom—freedom of the mind from constraint and indoctrination, to question and inquire and speak; freedom of the economy from corrupt and pervasive mismanagement; freedom of women from male oppression; freedom of citizens from tyranny—that underlines so many troubles of the Muslim world.[8]

This is a horrible misreading about the role and place of freedom in Islam and in Qur'anic perspective. Though the author is one of the most renowned American scholars on Islam and Middle East, most of his observations on Islam and Muslims are either flawed or miscalculated by any standard of scholarly paradigms. That is why Edward Said called this type of scholarship on Islam and Muslims "Orientalism," which includes the inability to understand any major problem of Muslim or Third world countries. To say that under the secular and nationalist rule in Turkey, Turkish masses did not have enough freedom to do whatever they wish or like is an utter lie. Secular Turkey had fallen practically into dire economic circumstances before the Özal government. Bankruptcy of the many of the former Soviet republics had frightened the

Turkish masses to the point that they wanted to see some way out both spiritually and economically.

Fethullah Gülen was able to usher a new hope through his writings and preaching in the minds of millions of Turkish people, young and old, that a genuine revival of the human spirit was possible through deeper and broadminded interpretations of the holy Qur'an. It was possible for him because Gülen, who memorized the entire Qur'an in his youth and is highly versed in the field of hadith, has studied both Islamic sciences and modern sciences, and he knows very well the Arabic language and the popular psyche of people. For the ordinary Muslim masses, it is not at all easy to comprehend the underlying spirit of the Qur'anic verses. It is rather very easy to be confused by the linguistic difficulties in understanding the Qur'an in relation to the numerous hadiths narrated and compiled at different times and circumstances of history.

As I argued elsewhere,[9] the problem here is the corresponding relations between the content of law and its sanctions. Straightforward readings of some verses of the Qur'an, such as "as for the thief, both male and female, cut off their hands"[10] may surprise the careful reader of the Qur'an who does not take this in the context of the entire message. Moreover, *cutting off* has also been described as limiting or closing down the ability of thieves. For an orthodox Muslim mind, such an interpretation may not be acceptable at all. However, many moderate Muslims think that this is the right approach to know the inner meanings of the Qur'anic verses. H. Patrick Glenn, in his thoughtful book entitled the *Legal Tradition of the World*, writes: "The expression would be a type model, in the same way that cutting out the tongue can be seen as simply requiring enforced silence, thus allowing both adherence to the Koran and measures other than mutilation."[11]

With the compilation of hadiths, a tension seems to have grown between the apparent Qur'anic messages and written traditions of the Prophet complied by different Islamic schools of law (*madhhab*). The Qur'an contains more than six thousand verses out of which only a few hundred can be regarded as law-related. In a modern legalistic sense, the Qur'anic verses on legal issues are fewer than the instructive messages to the believers to discover the mysteries surrounding them. Demystification of the ideas of the Islamic law is no longer an easy task. It is not merely a matter of simple or complex explanation of the Qur'anic verses or hadiths.

Noah Feldman reflects upon this complicated and complex issue of extrapolation of the Qur'anic interpretation and its connection to the implementation of those rules in the administration of justice:

> But if Shari'ah is popular among many Muslims in large part because of its historical association with the rule of law, can it actually do the same work today? Here there is reason for caution and skepticism. The problem is that the traditional Islamic constitution rested on a balance of powers between a ruler subject to law and a class of scholars who interpreted and administered that law. The governments of most contemporary majority-Muslim states, however, have lost these features. Rulers govern as if they were above the law, not subject to it, and the scholars who once wielded so much influence are much reduced in status. If they have judicial posts at all, it is usually as judges in the family-law courts.[12]

Gülen avoided such a controversy of bringing back the *ulama* to the state power or even near to the state machinery directly. Instead of pledging a special position for the *ulama* in the state or society, Gülen advocates for a fair system of governance and judiciary based on a predictable electoral and democratic system. Gülen does not claim that only religious people were victim of mismanagement and corruption in the post-colonial period. He argues that all people living under any tyrannical rule are victims of serious injustice and that Islam can offer help to all, irrespective of race, religion, and national identity. Gülen has argued that Turkey needs the true justice very dearly. This is true for all other Muslim countries as well.

> If Muslims are not able to come into contact with one another
> and constitute a union, to work together to solve common
> problems, to interpret the universe, to understand it well, to
> consider the universe carefully according to the Qur'an, to
> interpret the future well, to generate projects for the future, to
> determine their place in the future, then I do not think we can
> talk about an Islamic world.[13]

For Gülen, the Islamic world no longer exists in terms of
Muslim creativity and activism through which ordinary Muslims
can seek solutions in real mundane life. With the absence of such
dynamism in solving problems in life, no ideal society can be built
and thus no real Islam can be imagined. Gülen has been preaching
these messages at a time when most religious leaders and activists
have been indulging primarily in rhetorical aspects of Islamic theology or philosophy that have completely different purposes at different times. Many Muslim leaders still cannot fully realize that
Muslim nations are in grave crisis, and they need to act to solve
burning problems rather than creating new issues of ideological or
theological disputes that can never be solved by introducing categorical decisions in a fashion similar to the verdicts of courts.

In the past, the Muslim elite governing the masses under their
control needed some kind of codified laws and case-laws produced
by *qadi* (judicial) system deemed to be separate and independent
from the exercise of executive powers. The tensions between the literary meaning of the Qur'an and the *hikma* (wisdom) contained in
the *hadith*s led to a kind of separation of powers at different levels
of the Muslim polity and governance during the Abbasid period
(750–1258).

It is a typical problem with many Muslim religious scholars
that they like to hide their problems rather than trying hard to solve
those problems. This has been a case of legacy since the door of *ijtihad* was closed for the mainstream Muslim *ulama*. Gülen shows his
boldness to identify this central problem in Islamic theology and
has invited his fellow preachers to come up with solutions for the
problems by reutilizing the tool of independent reasoning in the

light of the Qur'an and Sunna. In this regard, he did not blame any particular type of Muslim or ethnicity; he has criticized all kinds of Muslim leaders representing all different kinds of Muslim civilizations. Gülen believes that the intellectual problems Muslim nations are experiencing now began almost one thousand years ago and then gradually engulfed the entire Muslim *ummah* as a disease of stagnation, destructive hostility, and extreme antagonism:

> This started with the Abbasid Era and with the appearance of the Seljukids. It increased after the conquest of Istanbul. In the period that followed, doors to new interpretations were closed. Horizons of thought became narrowed. The breadth that was in the soul of Islam became narrowed. More unscrupulous people begun to be seen in the Islamic world; people who were touchy, who could not accept others, who could not open themselves to everyone. The narrowness was experienced in the dervish lodges, as well. It is sad that it was even experienced in the *madrasa*s (school of theology). And of course, all of these tenets and interpretations require revision and renovation by cultivated people in their fields.[14]

Despite all kinds of criticism of the existence of five different schools[15] within Islamic jurisprudence, the diverse systems and methodologies succeeded in keeping Muslim societies competitive in production, distribution, and consumption. However, their collaboration and cooperation with governmental machineries were very selective and progressive in character. It is unbelievable that the Hanafi and Maliki schools had developed their own interpretations of the sources of Islamic jurisprudence almost in isolation from governmental involvement and interruptions. At some stage in their life, the founders of most schools of law were persecuted by Muslim governors because of the inconvenience the ruling elite faced as a result of their elaborate interpretations of the Qur'an and *hadith*s. Subsequently, the Muslim ruling elite in many regions of the Muslim world adopted one particular *madhhab* for the legitimacy of governance, and the Hanafi School received the most prominence. As a school of jurisprudence, the Hanafi *madhhab* is more formalist and methodical in many areas of regulating disputes and also appealing to the popular sentiments of a believer in performing rituals.

Gülen follows the Hanafi School, but has never tried to make it more rigid. It is his broad-mindedness and lenience that has attracted so many young and old Turkish people to become serious about Islamic traditions and values.

Gülen does not advocate the adoption of a particular *madhhab* at the state level, neither does he argue for the revival of the *qadi* system for establishing Islamic law and justice. Gülen has been very careful not to misplace any basic concept of Islamic justice in the political thinking process of Muslim politicians and the Muslim masses. This makes him very unique among his contemporary Islamic thinkers or religious scholars.

> The Economist stated that this "Turkish-based movement sounds more reasonable than most of its rivals and is vying to be recognized as the world's leading Muslim network." Comparing the Gülen movement with internationally established Muslim networks such as the Muslim Brotherhood, Hizb ut-Tahrir (Party of Liberation) and the Tablighi Jamaat of south Asian roots, The Economist commented that compared with all these groups that advocate a certain level of isolation from Western political life, the Gülen movement offers a message to young Muslims that sounds more positive. "It tells them to embrace the Western world's opportunities, while still insisting on Islam's fundamentals," the weekly said.[16]

Gülen's intellectual movement is unique because it does not provoke its ideological enemy to confront the supporters of the Gülen movement violently, and it is not a political movement. For example, nowhere has Gülen argued that Turkey needs to revive *qadi* system as a legal system to give an upper hand to religious scholars to administer justice. However, his call for justice and fairness for everybody based on the revealed sources is known to all. Unlike many Muslim scholars, Gülen does not think that Muslims need to avoid intratextual meaning of the Qur'anic revelation. The heavenly messages could not be successfully implemented in our lives without human reasoning and innovative ideas taking into consideration the specific context of situation and the time we are in. It is indeed the result of this approach that we see the development of the *fiqh* (rules of Islamic jurisprudence) and *ijtihad* (independent reasoning) during the early centuries of Islam.

Therefore, taken as a whole, we can come to a conclusion that the Qur'anic messages do not dictate any special type of state machinery as Gülen elucidates it clearly:

> In the Holy Qur'an, there are verses concerning administration and politics. The Prophet's practices also occupy an important place in this regard. For example, the Qur'anic terms *"ulu al-amr"* (those who rule), *"ita'at"* (obedience to the rulers), *"shura"* (consultation), *"harb"* (war), and *"sulh"* (peace), are all examples of some Qur'anic verses related to legal institutions and also some that point to politics and governing.
>
> However, in Islam it is not possible to limit the concept of governance and politics into a single paradigm, unlike the principles of faith and the pillars of Islam. History shows us that in the Muslim world, since the time of the Prophet, there have been many types of states.[17]

There is also very little scope for any particular clergy group to have a stronger role in running state affairs. However, historically many religious scholars have emerged as authorities by writing *tafsir*s (interpretations) of the whole Qur'an. After the emergence of a number of parallel Islamic schools, *tafsir* writing was regarded the most important way of serving Islam, though none of the founders of *madhhab*s wrote any *tafsir* in the typical sense. Individual interpretations of the Qur'anic verses ultimately have created more confusion among the Muslims than solving any major theological or political problems. Asma Barlas points out that,

> These [*tafsir*] texts have come to eclipse the Qur'an's influence in most Muslim societies today, exemplifying the triumph not only of some texts over others in Muslim religious discourse but also of history, politics, and culture over the sacred text, and

thus also of the cross-cultural, transnational, and nondenomina-
tional ideologies on women and gender in vogue in the Middle
Ages over the teachings of the Qur'an.[18]

Today millions of Arab and non-Arab Muslims read the Qur'an
every day, but they hardly dare or try to discover or rediscover any
substantial new meaning in it because they believe that everything
is set and the Qur'an has been defined for them explicitly. Moreover,
most of the Qur'anic studies have very little to do with syntactical
structures and principles and the organic linkages or relationship
between them. In the absence of a thorough creative synthesis of
the Qur'anic principles, and the interrelationship between them, in
many cases the spirit of the Qur'anic messages has been lost from
the mainstream Muslim population.

One manifestation of such a rigid thought process is the belief
in many Muslim societies that we have to follow the early *caliph*s or
*imam*s without being critical to their adopted decisions. Islamically
speaking, after the Prophets no one deserves such blind imitation.
Moreover, blind imitation is neither prophetic nor Islamic.
Explanations through both intra-textual and extra-textual interpretations of the Qur'anic messages are therefore very important in
discovering the hidden dimensions of the Prophetic mission to humanity. This point is clearly underlined in the following quote:

> The Prophetic actions of leadership, which are not based on the
> revelation, are special partial actions related to managing the
> status and the policy of the society, in a special time, place, and
> circumstances....When Prophet Muhammad, peace and bless-
> ings be upon him, was transmitting Allah's words or clarifying
> matters of religion, he did so according to what was divinely
> inspired; whereas when he made a decision as an *imam* or a
> political leader, he always worked according to his personal
> reasoning (*ijtihad*)....Consulting his Companions in his deci-
> sions is a further evidence that the Prophet's actions as an *imam*
> were based on personal reasoning. If the issue had been a matter
> of divine inspiration, he would not have resorted to consulta-
> tion. Actually, he listened to their opinions, consulted experts,
> and contemplated and discussed matters willingly....Muslim

constitutional jurists (ancient and contemporary alike) agree that the Ummah or the people is the origin of legitimacy for the state. Prophet Muhammad himself, peace and blessings be upon him, died without appointing a successor. He, peace and blessings be upon him, totally left the matter for people not only to select the person they want, but also to choose the method of selection. Such action on the part of the Prophet constitutes a meaningful constitutional precedent.[19]

The Umayyads, dominating the political and military powers (661–750) of the early Muslims, virtually disobeyed this fundamental Islamic and Prophetic constitutional principle but did not succeed in changing any extra-textual rulings that prohibits kings or heads of the states to retain absolute powers in their hands. The Abbasids, though, reversed the course of that absolutism but could not establish the principles of the prophetic traditions of governance in the spirit of intrinsic values of Islam. However, with the establishment of a number of paralleled Shi'i and Sunni *madhhab*s and collection of *sahih sittah* (six authentic collections) *hadith*s during early stage of Abbasid Caliphs, a kind of political pluralism existed up to the final fall of the Abbasids in 1258.

Under the pluralistic political climate sustained by the Abbasids, the Fatimids were able to take over the state power in Egypt (969–1171) and virtually controlled the holy cities in Mecca and Medina. From the center of political and military power in Baghdad, the Abbasids tried hard to overthrow the Fatimids in Egypt, but neither party could call the opposition an illegitimate or anti-Islamic government. Under the Fatimids, the Al-Azhar University in Cairo had become the most important Islamic seat of learning for both Sunnis and Shi'is, while Baghdad remained the center of political and military power for the entire Muslim *ummah* up to 1258. The Qur'an was better understood by Muslim masses during that time of ideological conflicts between Shi'is and Sunnis, and Arabs in general did not even try to sell any nationalistic and ethnic messages wrapped in "Islamic cloths."

Attempts to give the Qur'an ethnically-based meanings were not new in the Islamic history, but with the rise of nationalism in the nineteenth century, the Qur'an had received more Arabicized interpretations than under the rule of the centralized Muslim governance from Damascus (661–750) or Baghdad (750–1258). Arabs in general accepted the political and military leadership of the Ottomans from fourteenth to nineteenth century, and only with the rise of nation-state, history witnessed a non-spiritual reading/study of the Qur'an by people like Abdul Wahhab (d.1792), Mawdudi (1903–1979) and many others. Many believe that the famous medieval Hanbali scholar Ibn Taymiyya (d. 1328) established a strong line of "materialistic" or merely linguistic reading of the Qur'an. By the same token, many think that Mawlana Jalaluddin Rumi (1207–1273) established the line of the "spiritualistic" reading of the Qur'an.

This is a very old-age dichotomy associated with the study of the Qur'an, which assumes that one can take any meaning of its text depending upon his or her ability to read the "Mind of God." This problem becomes much more complicated when an interpreter believes or thinks that he has the best ability to know the hidden and implicit messages of the Qur'anic verses because of his linguistic and/or analytical skills. Such an arrogance and ignorance is completely *haram* (forbidden) in Islam. However, authors like Mawdudi and Ibn Wahhab claimed that they knew the best way to draw the line definitely and conclusively between Muslims with authentic faith and Muslims with pseudo-authentic ones:

> To ibn Abd al-Wahhab, the state of the Muslim community around him was nothing short of a reversion to the old polytheism, which the Qur'an and the Prophet condemned and sought to eliminate. Much of the debate surrounding early Wahhabi doctrine addressed the questions of what monotheism entails and whether nominal belief without more is sufficient to make one a Muslim.[20]

Such a strategy is nothing short of playing God in the name of Islam, telling people that heavenly grace is unlimited and the doors of mercy from God are always open and anyone can take benefit of any earthy and heavenly avenues for his or her spiritual salvation. However, authors using the Qur'anic verses try to identify the acts that could be accounted for *shirk* (associating partners with God) to reserve hell for those who commit that gravest sin and to find a guaranteed place in heaven for themselves. Such an attitude also might not be a big deal if such exponents of the Islamic law could focus on the issues only as a matter of theological discourse, but they bring it to the political and legal fields and try to wage a crusade against all sinners.

A major reason why many Muslim theologians take an anti-Islamic stand to draw conclusive lines between the people who will be going to hell or heaven is due to their unwillingness or incapability to differentiate between sins and crimes. Moreover, religious leaders argue that by changing the laws of the land, they would be able to diminish the difference between the concepts of sins and crimes. Islam is commonly described as a complete code of conduct from cradle to grave and thus could abolish all laws inherited from different kinds of un-Islamic sources and/or existing anti-Islamic rule. This is a thought of strict ideological nature, not a Qur'anic legal tool to discover all legal systems Muslims may develop or encounter in their religious mission for the quest of happiness or decent and honest livelihood on earth.

Here we can see how distinct the voice of Gülen is regarding political and religious discourse and in showing no intention to prefer one national pride over others. He does not propagate that a particular nation or state would be able to change the overall Islamic climate and religious values within a state boundary and beyond. This goes against the idea that an Islamic state can be established within a nation-state system. Gülen's appreciation of the globalization process and its consequences is very clear in his thoughts and writings.

> Modern means of communication and transportation have transformed the world into a large global village. So, those who expect that any radical changes in a country will be determined by that country alone and remain limited to it are unaware of current realities. This time is a period of interactive relations. Nations and people are more in need of and dependent on each other, a situation that causes closeness in mutual relations.[21]

An incorruptible political and legal mechanism to ensure an honest and adequate livelihood for all is the pre-condition for the establishment of a healthy society. A lack of these has led societies to become easy prey to endemic crimes and moral degradation. That has exactly happened with many contemporary Muslim countries. Still most religious circles have been ignoring this vital issue of Islamic justice and indulge in never ending theological discourse on *shirk*.

Drummond notes that, "It is said that God does not forgive the sin of ascribing associates to God. This is 'a mighty sin'. This language, we should note, is to be taken seriously but, as with many Koranic statements, we must place it in its larger context; in this case the larger context is the mercy and compassion of God, who does forgive the sins of all who seek his forgiveness."[22]

Instead of using the Qur'an to achieve mercy and guidance from heavenly sources, many Muslims tend to discover all different kinds of legal rules in the Qur'an to hold power and to abolish all existing un-Islamic or anti-Islamic rules in any particular society. Such an attitude practically goes against the very essence of all Qur'anic teachings that neither God nor the Prophet should be treated as an armed guard ready to destroy Muslims and non-Muslims alike at the time they commit sins.

The corner stone of justice based on the Qur'an is the protection of common or public good. It had created a heated debate among Muslim jurists how to determine the boundaries of public good and relate the spheres of individual duties toward different areas of public interests. Both the Maliki and Hanafi schools were uncompromising in regard to the common good, while the Shafi'i and

Hanbali schools put more emphasis on personal piety.[23] As human beings are ultimately responsible only to God for their actions, the concern for common good at the individual level cannot determine the degrees of grace or curse a person deserves on earth and heaven. But without a conducive public and social atmosphere, religious piety at the personal level becomes problematic and at times appears irrelevant to human existence and living. The Qur'anic messages are there to strike a balance between personal piety and duties toward collective or public life.

It was not an accident that many Muslims who converted to Islam during the early period of the Qur'anic revelation were either slaves or have-nots of the Arabian Peninsula. Moreover, slaves and women were more eager to embrace the Islamic messages derived from the Qur'an because such messages are based on *adl* (heavenly measures of justice). The average Arabs at the time did not need to read or know the interpretation of the Qur'an, they had just listened to the recitation of the Revelation[24] and captured the essence of it to change their life-styles and belief-system. Subsequently, history has witnessed that both Arab and non-Arab Muslims of early generations could follow the core teachings of Islam without giving much attention to the linguistic complexities of many complicated Qur'anic verses.

Gülen is absolutely correct to state that "the Qur'an came to change not one or two habits; it came to change everything: ways of living and dying, marrying, buying and selling, settling disputes, and how to perceive one's relation with the Creator, among others....The Qur'an was revealed in stages so that its audience could understand, internalize, and apply its prohibitions, commands, and reforms."[25] Under the leadership of the Prophet, Arab tribal society experienced comprehensive legal, economic, and social reforms. As a result, the scope of tribal polices had already been diminished. One would wonder how Islam could be so different from all other ideologies and religions in regard to so many issues, including racial and gender issues, so long ago when humanity had not achieved the intellectual maturity that we witness today in the twenty-first century.

It is true that unlike many other religions, Islam comprises all aspects of life and is very relevant to many political and mundane issues. However, to say that Islam is simply based on some political doctrines is mere ignorance about the inner truths of universal religion of Islam. In relation to the place of politics and the state administration in the Qur'an Gülen says:

> It would not be a correct understanding of Islam to claim that politics is a vital principle of religion and among its well established pillars. While some Qur'anic verses are related to politics, the structure of the state, and the forms of ruling, people who have connected the import of the Qur'anic message with such issues may have caused a misunderstanding. This misunderstanding is the result of their Islamic zeal, their limitations of their consideration solely of historical experiences, and their thinking that the problems of Islamic communities can be solved more easily through politics and ruling. All of these approaches within their own contexts are meaningful. However, the truth does not lie in these approaches alone.
>
> Although one cannot ignore the effects of ruling and administration in regulating communal relationships between individuals, families and societies, yet these, within the framework of Qur'anic values, are considered secondary issues. That is because the values that we call major principles (*ummuhat*), such as faith (*iman*), submission (*islam*), doing what is beautiful (*ihsan*), and the acceptance of divine morals by the community, are references that form the essence of administrative, economic, and political issues. The Qur'an is a translation of the book of the universe, which comes from the divine commands of creation, an interpretation of the world of the unseen, of the visible and invisible. It is an explanation of the reflections of the divine names on earth and in the heavens. It is a prescription for the various problems of the Islamic world. It is a unique guide for bliss in this life and in the life to come. It is a great guide for the travelers in this world moving towards the hereafter. It is an inexhaustible source of wisdom. Such a book should not be reduced to the level of political discourse, nor should it be considered a book about political

theories or forms of state. To consider the Qur'an as an instru-
ment of political discourse is a great disrespect for the Holy
Book and is an obstacle that prevents people from benefiting
from this deep source of divine grace.

There is no doubt that the holy Qur'an, through its enrichment of the human soul, is able to inspire wise politicians and
through them to prevent politics from being like gambling or
merely a game of chess.[26]

Unfortunately, many Muslim scholars tend to ignore the fact
that over emphasis on only political dimensions of Islam may lead
to serious confusion about the deeper spiritual senses of Islam that
constitute the foundation of Islamic civilization and legal reforms.

The Peaceful Spirit of Islam

Every civilization or religion wishes to guard itself from wicked
people or evil forces that try to destroy it. Islam cannot be an exception to this universal truth. Thus it is very natural that someone
would find isolated Qur'anic verses or sayings of the Prophet that
would justify a proportional use of force against the enemies of
truth, nature, and people. The followers of falsehood otherwise
would destroy the entire humanity and civilization.

Explaining the 61st verse of the *Sura at-Tawba*, Asad identifies
the enemies of Islam as the enemies of truth.[27] In various verses,
God Almighty warns the believers that there will always be enemies
of God and believers. Therefore, in the 60th verse of the *Sura al-
Anfal*, for instance, Muslims are asked always to be on the alert
against the enemies of truth and make ready whatever they can of
force against the enemy. Even such readiness is for deterrence, thus
building a lasting peace. The next verse is especially important as it
asks Muslims to incline towards peace if the enemy inclines to
peace. In explanation to this verse Ali Ünal puts forward, "it is stated that Muslims are peaceful and that they must live peacefully and
be representatives of universal peace."[28] In fact, the Islamic principles, including acting as a deterrent in the power balance, constitute

the foundation of "positive action," which goes deeper than simply avoiding any kind of unjust aggression. A Muslim is, indeed, a representative of peace, treating everyone kindly, Muslim and non-Muslim alike if they do not show enmity toward Islam:

> *God does not forbid you, as regards to those who do not make war against you on account of your Religion, nor drive you away from your homes, to be kindly to them, and act towards them with equity. God surely loves the scrupulously equitable.* (Qur'an 60:8)

Building a lasting peace is essential in Islam, and all kinds of unjust aggression are prohibited. Through the peaceful spirit of Islam and without violence or clashing with other civilizations and religions, Muslims are called to convey the Divine messages peacefully for the sake of upholding truth, prosperity, and enlightenment for the entire human race.

However, under the influence of modern tribalism and nationalism, Islamic principles and even the Qur'an itself have received a lot of misguided interpretations. But misinterpretation of the Qur'anic verses alone could not put the Muslim nation-states into the horrible situation they are in. Using the Qur'anic verses to support their arguments, some Muslim scholars believe that the creation of Israel or secular Muslim societies is the greatest sign of Muslim decadence and military failure of Muslim nations, while the establishment of "Islamic" Pakistan or Saudi Kingdom is the greatest blessing for the entire Muslim *ummah*. Such a misreading of the messages of the Qur'an and contemporary Muslim history has a serious impact on the modern Muslim psyche that in turn plays an important role in shaping Muslim political and intellectual consciousness.

Some nationalist forces wanted to get rid of misinterpretation of the Qur'anic verses by banning the use of religious issues at state levels. The constitutional principle of separation between church and state was sold to the Muslim media and public opinion without looking more deeply into the possible implementations of this idea. Hard-line secularism in some Muslim countries such as Turkey and

Egypt has opted for a coercive atheism and anti-Islamic propaganda to defeat Islamic forces in the struggle for political power. Moreover, secularism was used to justify many extra-judicial killing and systematic torture in the prison cells throughout the Muslim world.

Thus the introduction of secularism at state levels has practically ignited the fuel of religiosity in many Muslim societies. For many Muslims, secularism is akin to colonialism. Islamic belief enabled the Muslims to fight the colonial subjugation against foreign colonizers. Since the end of the typical European military colonialism, Islam has been used to defeat communist movements in many Muslim countries. In this backdrop, one has to analyze the tendencies of using the Qur'anic verses for reformist or *jihadi* movements. David Brooks of *New York Times* notes that majority of the radicals are educated, affluent, and professional modern individuals:

> We have learned a lot about the jihadists, from Osama bin Laden down to the Europeans who attacked the London subways last month. We know, thanks to a database gathered by Marc Sageman, formerly of the C.I.A., that about 75 percent of anti-Western terrorists come from middle-class or upper-middle-class homes. An amazing 65 percent have gone to college, and three-quarters have professional or semiprofessional jobs, particularly in engineering and science. Whether they have moved to Egypt, Saudi Arabia, England or France, these men are, far from being medieval, drawn from the ranks of the educated, the mobile and the multilingual. The jihadists are modern, psychologically as well as demographically, because they are self-made men (in traditional societies there are no self-made men). Rather than deferring to custom, many of them have rebelled against local authority figures, rejecting their parents' bourgeois striving and moderate versions of Islam, and their comfortable lives.[29]

Obviously, these radicals who are indeed strongly integrated to the modern life are radicals not because of religious piety but because of their political beliefs.

The Qur'an undoubtedly plays an important role in shaping and reshaping Muslim psyche and behavior. However to say that the Qur'an wishes to destroy the followers of other religions, non-believers, and atheists is a grossly mistaken interpretation. The anger and frustration many Muslims have expressed during last several centuries is the outcome of prolonged injustice inflicted on them by Western powers. Moreover, secular elites in the Muslim world have failed miserably to adhere to the tenets of Islam that have been preserved by ordinary Muslim masses through the ages at the cost of many supreme sacrifices. Secularists are the most corrupt segment of the population in many Muslim countries[30] and do not give much attention to the burning issues confronting their constituencies. The rise of the recent fundamentalist trend in many Muslim countries is mainly a reaction to the Western domination and prolonged exploitation of the Muslim world. Moreover, the rise of religious fundamentalism is now regarded as a global phenomenon, an outcome contributed largely by the failure of socialist ideologies to meet the minimum standard of life for the masses. A scrutiny of world events in a religious-historical perspective should make it clear that the Islamic causes for building a morally and ethically decent nation and even humankind would be better served by not allowing fundamentalist forces (secular and religious) to capture state powers. However, that needs to be done by peaceful means with the establishment of the principle of co-existence with all religions and values for building a better humanity for all races, creeds, and cultures.

> [I]t would not be right for anyone to claim that they have come up with a perfect interpretation of the endless content of this expository atlas of humankind, the universe and the truth of Divinity. The Qur'an can be interpreted only to the extent that a heavenly and Divine word can be interpreted by human perception....The Qur'an has captivated everyone to whom its voice has reached – provided they were not prejudiced – with its holistic perspective, comprehensive discourse and style, the vastness of its content and meaning, its delicate expressions, its magical expounding in proportion to the different levels of knowledge and understanding, and its capacity to penetrate souls. Neither its friends nor its foes have been able to come up

with something in a similar style or an utterance that is equal in grandiosity, the former motivated for imitation, the latter in fury to choke off its voice, despite their efforts for almost fourteen centuries, even when they use the same material and concentrate on the same issues.[31]

The lack of intellectual depth and the spiritual quagmire that many Muslim societies and communities find themselves in have prevented Muslims in general from delving into the deeper meanings of Qur'anic linguistic expressions and their significance for themselves and their non-Muslim counterparts. Most of the Qur'anic expressions are very strong in their utterance when they warn the wicked and mischievous quarters of a society or humankind. However, that does not mean that Muslims have to establish their societies based on fear and intimidation, rather Muslims are duty bound to discover and rediscover civilized ways and means to combat crimes and vices of any existing system without hurting the sensibilities of other segments of the population. In turn, Muslim societies deserve to be reciprocated with regard to this gesture, their voices heard and their systems of thought, beliefs, and governance recognized and respected. Muslims, in turn, need to understand the Qur'anic message appropriately. One can count about 600 verses in the Qur'an that are directly or indirectly related to formal legal issues that regulate and/or control human behavior. At the same time, the holy Qur'an urges the rich and powerful sections of the population to take care of needy and destitute more than 600 times, and it obliges Muslims to take all necessary legal steps to fulfill this core religious duty to others: *"in their wealth is a definite share for the asker and the ones who are needy"* (Dhariyat 51:19). Many Muslims believe that here the Qur'an has been referring to only *zakat*, i.e. a compulsory 2.5 percent yearly "purifying" tax on wealth to be distributed to the poor. However, the Qur'an goes much further beyond that mandatory binding of distributing only 2.5 percent of the wealth of the rich to the poor. The basic teaching of Islam about the ideal Muslim society is that nobody should remain hungry, illiterate, or destitute. It is a prime responsibility for every Muslim government and society to provide quality education to all men and women living within its territory or under its jurisdiction. For their part, each Muslim man and woman should try to get adequate and appropriate education to lead an honest and dignified life up to the end of his or her time on earth. Unlike many traditional Muslim religious scholars, Gülen's approach to the Qur'an and building an ideal society for all is neither rigid nor exclusive. Gülen stands for an inclusive society based on universal human values. Gülen does not see any conflict between the fundamental teachings of the Qur'an and the inherent nature of the human race to be elevated spiritually and materially and dignified on earth and in the Hereafter.

CHAPTER 5

Gülen's Notion of *Hizmet* and Public Good: From a Strategy to an Action Plan

GÜLEN'S NOTION OF *HIZMET* AND PUBLIC GOOD: FROM A STRATEGY TO AN ACTION PLAN

Hizmet [literally, "service"] for Gülen implies that a person devotes his or her life to Islam, serving for the benefit of others, which is beneficial for life after death. Gülen is a very restless person who is always asking himself if he might do more for God. Death is always present in his preaching to his followers, and the fear of judgment day is the motivation to work hard.[1]

Muslim activists have been broadly divided into traditionalists with an apparent orthodox blend and Islamists with radical views of changing politics. However, deeper understanding of Islamic spiritual teachings and adherence to them makes the dividing line between these two groups blurred for non-specialists. For quite some time, many specialists have been speculating how the history of the Gülen movement would look like in the annals of the revival of Islamic heritage, including Sufism and social activism. Some observers claim that Gülen is a traditional *alim* (Islamic scholar); others say that he is a modern Sufi. Many critics tend to claim that he is neither a religious scholar nor a traditional Sufi, but a modern Islamic propagandist and preacher.[2] These conflicting opinions on the identity of Gülen and the substance of his preaching is not due to the peculiarities and/or style of Gülen's writing but because of contrasting ideas about Islamic theology, politics, and Sufism.

As Zeki Saritoprak notes, "One can say that Sufism was to Islamic law what Jesus was to Hebrew law. In time, some Sufis went too far, underestimating and even neglecting some basic religious law, which resulted in the emergence of extreme, esoteric movements. The debate continues between fundamentalist Wahhabi Muslims and Sufis even today."[3]

For a long time, many prominent Muslim scholars were also in bewilderment as to how to strike a balance between orthodox interpretations of Islamic tenets and strict adherence to them, on the one hand, and liberal interpretations and observance of the Islamic way of life, on the other. In other words, how to remain a devout Muslim at personal levels and attain a compassionate attitude toward others in regard to religious obedience at public places and in dealing with cultural matters of common interests. Gülen's position on these matters is quite unique. His writings sound like orthodox interpretations of Islamic tenets, but his practical approach is very flexible and realistic, distinguished with love and compassion in treatment of others. Saritoprak nicely summarizes Gülen's unique stance of Sufism:

> Gülen's way of Sufism cannot be confined by the framework of a specific Sufi order. Strictly speaking, Gülen is not a Sufi. However, in light of Hujwiri's definition quoted earlier, Gülen is a Sufi in practice, if not in name...Gülen can be called a Sufi, albeit a Sufi in his own way.[4]

SOLVING THE PARADOX: HOW TO BE A BALANCED MUSLIM

This is Gülen's most unique achievement. He did not give up his own religious practice in any areas of his activities and also extended his cooperation and collaboration with many other peaceful groups of activists dedicated to good works of social progress and cultural enlightenment. A major problem with the orthodox Islamic interpretation is that it gives too much importance to outer aspects of Islamic rituals at the cost of inner values ingrained in them. As a result, many religious groups have become simply ritualistic in their behaviors and tend to ignore responsibility toward society at large and their fellow citizens in particular.

Critics of Islamic religiosity argue that if you become devout Muslim, then you ultimately lose interest in building humane society; contrary to this view, many others say that Islamic activism ultimately make Muslims radical in their political behavior. It is true that some people who are "Sufis" only in name have become indifferent to the miseries of others. Political activists in many Muslim societies are either too engaged in religious matters or insensitive to the economic and social needs of others.

Gülen transmits Islamic tenets in a way that everyone can see a role for himself and herself in building a compassionate society where all human beings can co-exist with one another for greater causes based on sacrifice and altruism. It is not an easy task to accomplish for a society where everyone is concerned only for his or her own material gain. Gülen has argued tirelessly that even for the material wellbeing, a Muslim must follow an Islamic way of life. However, one needs to ignite a fire of faith in his or her soul to keep a balance between material ambitions and spiritual goals. Exploring Gülen's thought, Yavuz finds the following aspects:

> Muslims constantly are reminded that avoiding sin is not enough; rather, engaging to create a more humane world is required. Salvation means not only to be "saved from" sinful activities, but also to be engaged actively in the improvement of the world. According to Gülen, moral consciousness toward other cultures can be raised only through participating in an action. In a way, becoming morally upright person (*insan-i kamil*) is possible only through morally informed conduct.[5]

It is a primary duty for every adult Muslim to try not to engage in any sinful dealings and acts. However, if a societal and state system is based on wide capitalism, extreme communism, or vulgar consumerism, then for a regular person it is quite difficult to escape from sinful deals and activities on a regular basis. As a result, a vast majority of Muslims have either abandoned the so-called puritanical Islamic norms and values, or they have become very pessimistic in their attitude to the national building process and ongoing creative activities for the pursuit of scientific discoveries and innovative use of the expanding horizons of technology.

Gülen has envisioned new ideas and interpretations of Islamic tenets that invite people in general and Muslims in particular to discover fine lines between extreme materialism and unproductive spiritualism. To Islam, worldly life is like a farm land from which a Muslim needs to collect his new capital to be invested for the eternal life after death. The path of spiritual salvation is very much individualistic in nature, but both the process of cultivation of farm land and the distribution of capital for the Hereafter is a collective endeavor for the fruition of faith in its every stage of mundane and spiritual life. For quite some time, an ordinary Turkish mind took Gülen as a simple follower and disciple of Bediüzzaman Said Nursi (1877–1960), whose writings,[6] of course, have played a very important role in placing Gülen in the line of peaceful preaching of universal Islam in the Turkish environment.

Gülen is, however, a dynamic preacher, social activist, and exponent of Islamic ideas, who pushes the boundaries of the Islamic message far beyond the parameters set by Nursi. Gülen has never underestimated the influence of Nursi on the Turkish religious mind and has held Nursi paradigm dearly in his effort to bring more and more Turks in the fold of value-based education for all irrespective of national or ethnic identities, race, religion, and gender.

> [O]wing to state political oppression, a new form of Islamic activism evolved out of the Ottoman-Turkish intellectual tradition. Said Nursi formulated a new way of religious renewal through collective reading circles, the *dershanes*, to raise religious consciousness...One can identify Nursi's writings as the foundational text for Fethullah Gülen because Gülen always has used Nursi's method of raising Islamic consciousness and the reading circles to create transnational religious networks.[7]

Whenever the Islamic consciousness leading to activism and intellectual discourse is the subject of consideration, many critics talk about "political" Islam based on tribalism and antagonistic politics for the pursuit of capturing state power and money market. However, for Gülen, Islam is not a "political project" to be implemented. If the Nur movement, inspired by the writings of Bediüzzaman Said Nursi, was purely ritualistic and somehow Turkish in nature, then Gülen is very much outward looking in terms of his ideas about cosmopolitanism and internationalism. However, this difference might not be of fundamental nature between Nursi and Gülen as the latter has had more means available and is thus able to make use of these greater means in today's world.

For an Islamic preacher of Gülen's stature, the Turkish context was not able to be friendly at all, especially few decades ago. But Gülen has used every heaven-sent opportunity to reach out to everyone at home and abroad. For Gülen, national pride should not be a hindrance to become a true Muslim, nor should it stand in the way of participation in transnational endeavors that benefit of humankind as a whole. Such an inclusive nature of Gülen's preaching brought him prominence rather quickly amongst his Turkish constituencies and beyond. Gülen's call for value-based education was an open invitation for all, and it really meant for the enrichment of human soul for the benefits of others.

Because of many misconceptions about fate-related verses in the Qur'an and Hadith, practicing Muslims in general tend to become fatalist in their thinking and are rather quite reluctant to make enough efforts to bring about positive changes for the masses. Misery and hardship constantly threaten the life and dignity of ordinary people of all races, nationalities, and genders. Such a situation has been taken as a destiny of those helpless masses. This very pessimistic attitude has no place in Islamic consciousness. However, because of the overwhelming colonial exploitation and pro-longed internecine fighting between Muslim nations and ethnicities within them, even many devout Muslims accept such a horrible and unbearable situation acceptable to masses at large.

Gülen has taken the worldly life as an open book, which you can color according to your determination, capability, and circumstances. However, no one alone can give new height to this special creativity without active and generous help of others. Thus only sincere and collective efforts can make one's contribution to any area of science or education substantial and beneficial for others and surrounding entities.

As Yavuz argues, "Gülen is an inspirational leader of a transnational education movement, whereas Nursi was the formative giant of intellectual discourse. Although Nursi was focused on *personal* transformation, Gülen has focused on *personal* and *social* transformation by utilizing new liberal economic and political conditions."[8]

The traditional and orthodox forces within Islamic circles tend to act to maintain the *status quo*, and such a conservative attitude is quite harmful to the underprivileged and disadvantaged segments of any society and state. Apparently one needs to become a revolutionary to speak against such religious taboo or stigma. However, keeping himself within the fold of traditional religious circles, Gülen puts forward his ideas of social change through educational excellence to achieve new heights in Islamic consciousness.

GÜLEN'S STRATEGY: REALIZATION OF POTENTIAL IN A NON-REACTIVE WAY

For Gülen, if you are really interested in attaining the pleasure of God or wish to become an *insan al-kamil* (universal, perfected man), you need to sacrifice a lot for others in terms of time, energy, and resources. Without doing so, no one should think that he or she is a very good Muslim or human being dedicated to the causes of Islam and humanity. Many social or human rights activists and religious propagandists of all kinds tend to preach high-sounding morality and human values to others, but in practice they are no more than empty, voluble talkers or even voracious consumers and exploiters of cheap labors, domestic workers, and fellow worshippers and/or citizens.

Gülen has never been naïve about the self-righteous weakness of religious people in general and Muslims in particular. He has emerged as a symbol of emulation in the path of altruism, which is now regarded as one of the major features of Islamic activism in the field of education and dedication to the causes of humanity and humility. Gülen's rationality for using religious values or scientific discoveries and technology for the benefits of humanity is in touch with the socio-political context, on the one hand, and basic human values on the other.

As Kuru points out, "Ethics and moral principles, Gülen argues, are crucial for the real enlightenment of humans. To maintain harmony, peace, and happiness in human life requires the realization of both mental/rational and heart-based/spiritual enlightenment.... Gülen argues that reason and Islamic revelation are not only compatible, but also complementary."[9]

This is in fact a revolutionary message for many traditional religious circles, which tend to reject such a universal idea. As a rational entity, the human being cannot accept many natural phenomena without proper explanations that conceptualize them in terms of higher truths revealed to the human race throughout the revelation period. As the revelation period ended, so the role of reasoning has increased tremendously. Many experts on theology and social sciences simply do not give enough attention to the correlation between revealed texts and the process of enlightenment of human societies. As a result we find the religious forces at loggerheads with the secularists, who also might emerge as an equally dangerous force in terms of human rights and justice for all.

Many religious forces in the Muslim world have emerged as a political platform against western colonialism and imperialism. However, none of these religious groups were unable to play positive role for a long time because anti-colonial and anti-imperialist forces' actions were based mainly on reactionary strategies. As Enes Ergene's analysis indicates, the Gülen movement is fundamentally different; it is not a reactionary mobilization:

Orientalism was both exploitative and colonial. Islamist ideology was born, therefore, as a political identity opposed to exploitation...the Gülen movement is not a reactionary movement, and it has no relation to the alienated reactionarism.[10]

Gülen has acknowledged all evil deeds perpetrated on Muslims by the former imperialist forces, but has offered some new strategies to fight back against those neo-colonialist forces. First of all, unlike many of his contemporary religious leaders and preachers, Gülen has been highly sensitive to the suffering of common people for economic and social reasons. Usually, like other clergymen of non-Islamic traditions, Muslim religious figures always try to remain correct theologically or religiously and tend to ignore many social, economic, and cultural considerations to be genuinely righteous. Such a tendency has ultimately led many Muslim communities to a kind of seclusion, while Islam is primarily an inclusive religion.

Keeping the aspects of theological correctness under the paradigms of reasoning, Gülen reaches out to Muslims of all kinds, who have been suffering from identity crisis. Hard-line secularism and ultra-nationalism have forced Turkey in ideological antagonism and a deep identity crisis. Neither the orthodox religious circles nor the secularists could address this serious problem of identity crisis of Turks for quite some time. Making the issues of modernity and scientific discoveries relevant to religious thoughts, and vice versa, Gülen has proved himself a social activist and educationist, who offers younger generations diverse ways of fruitful interaction with other communities. He has spoken about Anatolian Muslimness, or the "Muslimness of Turkish people" and not an ethnic Turkish Islam, which is incompatible with his entire educational and spiritual movement.[11] Indeed, Gülen clearly distinguishes negative and positive dimensions of national identity. While expressing his disapproval of nationalism in the sense of racialism, which is nourished by devouring others and which persists through hostility towards other peoples, he draws attention to its positive dimension of mutual assistance and solidarity, which ensures a beneficial strength and is a means for further strengthening Islamic brotherhood.

In modern times, whenever Muslims talk about Islam, many believe that we want to focus on politicized religious ideas or ancient values of Islamic civilization, regarded as a backward looking ideology not compatible with modern way of life. On the other hand, modernity has been regarded as a system where most of the issues related to industrialization, urbanization, and feminism have been melted down in way that everything can co-exist and flourish for its own benefit. Thus some argue that religion is full of contradictions and conflicts while modernism is a suitable and functional system for all except for some religious fundamentalist groups. Gülen's social sensitivity and responsibility has proved that such a presumption is not true at all. However, his idea came under fire simultaneously from modernists and religious fanatics. Ergene summarizes the peculiar style of Gülen's alternative path as the following:

> His style was shaped in accordance with the socio-psychological demeanor of the society he was addressing. He would filter all his actions and words through the most sensitive screens before he revealed them...his policy was soon to be opposed by some conservative elements in his environment who were unable to calculate the long-term social results of educational projects and opening schools....One of the basic aims of the global education activities is to form bridges that will lead to dialogue between religions and civilizations.[12]

Thus the intellectual and spiritual undertaking Gülen pursues through his social and educational movements knows no border of national or ethnic identity, but has indeed addressed the problem of hollowness in religious beliefs with no action plans in life and the problem of modernity with extreme selfishness and vulgar consumerism. The project is a grandiose one, and with it Gülen has evolved as a social reformer of a special kind having a global impact.

For Gülen, no human being can justify his own power without serving people at large and fellow-citizens in particular. However, with a defeatist mentality nurtured through colonial education system, it is quite difficult for Muslims to put trust in the inherent strength of Islamic world views, like the duty of service to others. At the same time, the much claimed supremacy of the Islamic way of life cannot be established through any coercive method. This is the core Islamic message that should not be put under question; it is a kind of universal lesson to be put in practice all the times. Similarly, public good needs to be promoted and protected all the times and in every kind of human activities. Gülen's vision and mission are totally dedicated to the causes of humanity and public good that should be distributed among all irrespective of creed, culture, and gender:

> [We] consider the past as a living body that speaks for us, thinks for us, and whispers words for us. We see a world that speaks through streams, rivers, seas, hills, and plateaus. In reality, the future is a world where opportunities come one after another.[13]

Numerous similar statements by Gülen demonstrate that Gülen invites everyone to do good works for the future generations, who will ultimately shape the world according to their ability and pursuit of creativity and happiness. Muslims are duty-bound to act on this basic principle of and justification for human existence on earth.

CHAPTER 6

Gülen's Thoughts on
Modern Democracy

GÜLEN'S THOUGHTS ON
MODERN DEMOCRACY

We may call our age a modern and democratic era run by information technology. Religious thoughts and ideas have very little role to play in the secular world of the modern man, who is engaged in serious discoveries in science and technology. A modern intellectual mind strongly believes that one can easily undertake an empirical study on democratic system, rule of law, and human rights without being concerned about any serious spiritual and religious thoughts. Moreover, it is argued in most cases that religious issues are detrimental to the development of democracy and technology, and thus the constitutional ideas of separation of church from state has been regarded as a political solution to many economic and development problems.

Some Muslims, especially those from the countries with an overwhelming Muslim population, do not favor the Western democratic system because of its secular stance, on one hand, and their vision of political "Islamism," on the other. Turkey was the first Muslim country to take the constitutional principle of the separation of religious and civil affairs seriously and aggressively and to use state power to transform the society into one where religious sentiments are not tolerated. The constitution of Turkey establishes the country as a secular state which guarantees the freedom of religious exercise; however, secularism has been variously interpreted by those at different points on the Turkish political spectrum. The non-religious, hard-line secularists' version of secularism differs greatly from the traditional secularism of the West, where secularism means the separation of the church and state with an absolute freedom to religious beliefs and worship. The former's version of secularism is an illiberal model which allows no role whatsoever for faith in public life. The Turkish population was unhappy with their forceful introduction of this hard-line secularism and the ideological course of their society and state that holds that modernization will lead to the growing irrelevance of religious presence in the public sphere.

Like many other Muslim countries, some religious circles also tended to believe that along with secularism, democracy would destroy the very Islamic and Muslim cultural fabric of Turkish society. However, unlike the minority of fundamentalist Islamists who attack secularism and democracy or the minority of hard-line secularists who are harsh in their imposing of secularism on Turkish people as a way of life and radically laicist worldview, the vast majority of Turkish people, including conservative, practicing Muslims, do not have a problem with the secular, democratic, and social state based on the rule of law, remaining neutral on religious issues, and guaranteeing freedom to religious beliefs and worship.

In many social and political considerations, Islam can be regarded as an ideology to be followed for achieving concrete economic goals at global, national, and community levels. However, to say that Islam is an ideology very similar to that of democracy or socialism is a serious misconception about Islam. Not many Muslim religious leaders and scholars could successfully remove this intellectual confusion from the minds of Muslims as well as the adversaries of Islam. Gülen is an exception to this rule. In an interview with Hulusi Turgut from *Sabah* daily, Gülen said:

> Islam is a religion. It can't be called anything else. When the West defeated the Islamic world in military and technology, salvation was sought in politicizing Islam or transforming it into a political system. This resembles a modern version of Khawarij,[1] whereas Islam as a religion is based on enlightening the mind and brightening the heart. Thus faith and worship comes first. The fruit of faith and worship is morality.[2]

With the rise of Islamic revolutionary forces in many parts of the Muslim world, many believed that Turkey might also follow the suit of Islamic revolution to defy the century-long modern democratic tradition and electoral system. Religious leaders in Turkey have appeared with their deep-seated moderate voice of reconciliation between democracy and Islam. In intellectual and spiritual fronts, Gülen has championed the idea that we need to find new paradigms of peaceful coexistence between religious and democratic forces:

> On the issue of Islam and democracy, one should remember that the former is a divine and heavenly religion, while the latter is a form of government developed by humans. The main purposes of religion are faith (*iman*), servanthood to God (*'ubudiyyah*), knowledge of God (*ma'rifah*), and beautiful actions (*ihsan*). The Qur'an, in its hundreds of verses, invites people to faith and worship of the Truth (*al-Haqq*). It also asks people to deepen their servanthood to God in a way that they may gain the consciousness of *ihsan*. "To believe and do good deeds," is among the subjects that the Qur'an emphatically stresses.... [M]any speak of religion as tantamount to politics, which is, in fact, only one of the many faculties of religion. Such a perception has resulted in a range of positions on the subject of the reconciliation of Islam and democracy. Even if these terms are not seen as being opposites, it is evident that they are different in important ways.
>
> According to one of these conceptualizations, Islam is both a religion and a political system. It has expressed itself in all fields of life, including the individual, family, social, economical and political spheres. From this angle, to confine Islam to only faith and prayer is to narrow the field of its interaction and its interpenetration. Many ideas have been developed from this perspective and more recently these have often caused Islam to be perceived as an ideology. According to some critics, such an approach made Islam merely one of many political ideologies. This vision of Islam as a totalizing ideology is totally against the spirit of Islam, which promotes the rule of law and openly rejects oppression against any segment of society. This spirit also promotes actions for the betterment of society in accordance with the view of the majority.

Those who follow a more moderate pattern also believe that it would be much better to introduce Islam as a complement to democracy instead of presenting it as an ideology. Such an introduction of Islam may play an important role in the Muslim world through enriching local forms of democracy and extending it in such a way that helps humans develop an understanding of the relationship between the spiritual and material worlds. I believe that Islam also would enrich democracy in answering the deep needs of humans, such as spiritual satisfaction, which cannot be fulfilled except through the remembrance of the Eternal One....

Moreover, democracy is not an immutable from of governing. Looking at the history of its development, one can see mistakes which are followed by changes and corrections. Some have even spoken of thirty types of democracy. Due to these changes in the evolution of democracy, some have looked at this system with hesitancy. Maybe this is a reason why the Muslim world did not view democracy with great enthusiasm. Besides this lack of enthusiasm, the violence of despotic rulers in the Islamic world, who see democracy as a threat to their despotism, presents another obstacle for democracy in Muslim nations.[3]

In an interview with Nuriye Akman, Gülen stated that, "It is wrong to see Islam and democracy as opposites. In periods when Islam wasn't fully practiced, perhaps it was more backward than today's democracy. For example, human rights were stepped on and despotic persons headed the state." He further stated that, "Democracy is a system the world has favored, but it is still being refined. It's on the way to its real essence.... Democracy is a process; it's not possible to turn back."[4] In another interview, discussing the various manifestations of democracy, including Christian democrats, social democrats, and liberal democrats, Gülen asks why there should not be a democracy which includes Islamic sensibilities and thoughts, and he stresses that, "In a developed democracy, in the same way that a secular person should be provided with peace in this world, another person who believes in the hereafter should also be given an opportunity to experience the hereafter."[5] Gülen calls attention elsewhere to such a humane democracy that has a metaphysical dimension, embracing human beings with all of their aspects and fulfilling their spiritual needs:

> It is possible to envisage a kind of democracy with a spiritual dimension. It is a democracy which contains respect for and observance of human rights and freedoms, including freedom of speech, expression and religion, a democracy which prepares the necessary conditions for people to live and practice as they believe, which renders people able to fulfill their wish and need for eternity, and which takes or deals with human beings as a whole with regard to their all material and immaterial needs. For, human life does not start and end with life in this world; the world is only a temporal, transit station, and people are ceaselessly moving toward their eternal abode. The system that governs them must not ignore or neglect this crucial matter. We therefore have to seek ways to sophisticate and humanize democracy. No such stage or democracy has been attained yet, in east or west, north or south, but we can aspire to and work for such an aim.[6]

In answer to a question on the form of government Islam offers, Gülen says:

> Islam does not propose a certain unchangeable form of government or attempt to shape it. Instead, Islam establishes fundamental principles that orient a government's general character, leaving it to the people to choose the type and form of government according to time and circumstances. If we approach the matter in this light and compare Islam with today's modern liberal democracy, we will better understand the position of Islam and democracy with respect to each other.[7]

Gülen argues that democracy, in spite of its many shortcomings, is the only viable choice in modern times as a political and governing system that allows people to govern themselves. He bases this on the Qur'anic principle that individuals and societies are responsible for their own fate:

> As Islam holds individuals and societies responsible for their own fate, people must be responsible for governing themselves.

The Qur'an addresses society with such phrases as: "O people!" and "O believers!" The duties entrusted to modern democratic system are those that Islam refers to society and classifies, in order of importance, as "absolutely necessary, relatively necessary, and commendable to carry out." People cooperate with one another in sharing these duties and establishing the essential foundations necessary to perform them. The government is composed of all of these foundations.[8]

Supporting the compatibility of Islam and democracy, Gülen points out that the Qur'an addresses the whole community and assigns it almost all the duties entrusted to modern democratic systems:

Islam recommends a government based on a social contract. People elect the administrators and establish a council to debate common issues. Also, the society as a whole participates in auditing the administration....Islam is an inclusive religion. It is based on the belief in one God and Creator, Lord, Sustainer, and Administrator of the universe. Islam is the religion of the whole universe. That is, the entire universe obeys the laws laid down by God, so everything in the universe is "Muslim" and obeys God by submitting to His laws.[9]

ISLAM AND DEMOCRACY: ANALYTICAL CONFUSIONS AND CONCEPTUAL CLARIFICATIONS

The most problematic issue in the discussion of Islam and democracy is that many religiously oriented leaders and activists want to put God-made law in the place of man-made laws to prove that the Islamic laws are a solution to all secular problems human beings face every day. There are two main reasons for this dichotomy of thinking in terms legal systems. First, many believe that state sovereignty challenges God's sovereignty over the universe and humankind. In relation to this Gülen states:

The argument that is presented is based on the idea that the religion of Islam is based on the rule of God, while democracy is based on the view of humans, which opposes it. In my understanding, however, there is another idea that has become a victim of such a superficial comparison between Islam and democracy. The phrase, "Sovereignty belongs to the nation unconditionally," does not mean that sovereignty has been taken from God and given to humans. On the contrary, it means that sovereignty is entrusted to humans by God, that is to say it has been taken from individual oppressors and dictators and given to the community members. To a certain extent, the era of the Rightly-Guided Caliphs of Islam illustrates the application of this norm of democracy. Cosmologically speaking, there is no doubt that God is the sovereign of everything in the universe. Our thoughts and plans are always under the control of the power of such an Omnipotent. However, this does not mean that we have no will, inclination or choice. Humans are free to make choices in their personal lives. They are also free to make choices with regard to their social and political actions. Some may hold different types of elections to choose lawmakers and executives. There is not only one way to hold an election; as we can see, this was true even for the Era of Bliss, the time of the Prophet of Islam, and during the time of the Four Caliphs, may God be pleased with them all. The election of the first Caliph, Abu Bakr, was different than of the second Caliph, Umar. Uthman's election was different from that of Ali, the fourth Caliph. God only knows the right method of election.[10]

Elsewhere Gülen clearly states that there is no particular model in Islam for either the method of election or the system of administration and further elucidates the issue:

[W]hen we look into the historical development of the Islamic system of government, Abu Bakr was elected by the public; but Umar was elected after he was nominated by Abu Bakr. Uthman was elected after Umar indicated the group of *ashara al-mubashshara* (ten persons who had been given glad-tidings for Paradise), one of which was Uthman. There was some opposition to Ali's election, and another administration was formed in Damascus with an opportunity being born for Muawiya. During the Umayyad reign, rule began to be passed down from father to son, a practice which continued with the Ottomans. All this shows that the religion has certain commandments with a definite methodology; these have never been touched. Outside of this is a territory of relative truths that are open to interpretation (*ijtihad*) and judgmental inference (*istinbat*), so that the conditions and needs of the time should be duly evaluated.[11]

Secondly, in many Muslim countries secular forces tend to destroy the social cohesion and cultural harmony that preserves family life more than in most Western countries, and they sometimes do this in the name of "democracy." Turkey is one of the countries in which secular forces via the military interventions had proved to be directly detrimental to the rise of genuine democratic rule.

Despite the many gross examples of misuse and abuse of secularism and democracy in Turkey, Gülen had never lost hope in electoral system in Turkey. He is confident that once people are given freedom and right to choose comparatively honest people to run the country, then they will make the right decision. Moreover, Gülen tells his countrymen that all the nationalist and secular people also need the values of Islam if they wish to become real democrats to serve their people without indulging in massive corruption that had occurred throughout the government in Turkish politics up to the mid of 1980s:

> The Islamic social system seeks to form a virtuous society and thereby gain God's approval. It recognizes right, not force, as the foundation of social life. Hostility is unacceptable...If human beings are considered as a whole, without disregarding the spiritual dimension of their existence and their spiritual needs, and without forgetting that human life is not limited to this mortal life and that all people have a great craving for eternity, democracy could reach its peak of perfection and bring even more happiness to humanity. Islamic principles of equality, tolerance, and justice can help it do just that.[12]

In no Muslim society can democracy alone shape the fabric of social and cultural values that are embedded in the spiritual and religious climate inherited from Islamic traditions. Like Turkey, a number of Muslim countries had accepted democracy as a system to fix the political problems and disputes related to power sharing between warring factions based on their party affiliation and ethnic origin. For Gülen, a just political system based on democratic principles is not a problem for the Islamic social system and cultural values. As we have seen, the hard-line secularist and ultra-nationalist forces have not been able to solve the problem with Kurdish separatists, for example, because while applauding every non-religious method, they simply disregard the unifying Islamic values and traditions which indeed provide the essential basis for the solution of the separatist terror. As a result, Turkish human rights records under secular governments up to the end of 1980s was worsening, and with the change the country has gone through not only in the economic sphere but also in the areas of democratization, those records have started to improve gradually.

A conservative government with Islamic sensitivities coming to power in many Muslim countries has been regarded as a threat to the constitutional principle of the separation of religion and state. In any Western democracy, a formal separation between church and state is seen as an indispensable part of democracy because for many centuries, the church interfered with the state affairs negatively. In addition, due to the ongoing religious wars in the long history of Europe, "secularism became a necessity for civil peace and stability, and states soon refused to pursue any religious goals. The separation of the state and religion became the bedrock of the European state system, and secularism became the constitutive feature of modernity."[13]

Western and colonialist historians do believe that this was the case with the Muslim and Islamic civilization as well. However, the fact of the matter is that in general during the entire medieval era Islam played quite a progressive role in national building of many countries in many regions such as in the Arab Middle East, North Africa, Central Asia, Iran, Turkey, and in the Indian subcontinent.

European and imperial historians under different Western powers have already rewritten that history by using the paradigms of modern secularism that divorce religious and moral values from the state system, and school curricula have incorporated those concocted histories into the educational system thoroughly. Secular Turkey, along with the former Soviet Central Asian republics, was the worst victim of such manipulative methodology of imparting knowledge through a strictly controlled schooling system against Islam. The indoctrination disregarding Islam or rejecting any Islamic considerations has worked very well in many educational systems such as British, Soviet, and even Turkish systems. The hard-line secularist ideology that denies any religious presence in public life in Turkey has made the vast majority of Turkish people unhappy for a long time. Gülen is a voice that had established that Muslims should and can take this challenge intellectually and spiritually instead of making it a cause for ideological rift between Muslims and hard-line secularists. Gülen argues that there is no inherent conflict between religious devoutness and secularism: "Secularism should not be an obstacle to religious devoutness, nor should devoutness constitute a danger to secularism."[14]

Harsh Soviet or French secularism has been a serious threat to Muslim social and cultural values. The Soviets tried to compensate or neutralize that by adopting the values of socialist internationalism and multiculturalism. However, the atheistic features of Russian communism destroyed all gestures of the Soviets to neutralize anti-Islamism in the communist bloc. Moreover, the Soviet military intervention into Afghanistan in December 1979 destroyed all hopes for any long lasting reconciliation between Islam and socialism.

Similarly, the western roots of secularism can be problematic for societies whose other experience of imports from the West have been in terms of colonial and imperial domination. Since the colonial period in the Muslim world, religious segments have become disinterested in politics of their countries. Only the anti-Islamic character of imposed secularism and atheism that worried the Muslim masses ultimately led Muslim people to join politics under this or that religious and/or political parties. On the other hand

Gülen, who holds religion to be far above politics, has never been involved in any political activity and warns all participants of the movement against the desire of joining any political party directly. He stresses continually that the people in the movement are not motivated by fame, position, or money. Whatever they do in this transient world, he says, they should do all with the hereafter in mind and for the pleasure of God. Of course, he encouraged people to use their votes, seeing it a citizen's right and responsibility. He sees religion as a source of morality and ethics, which are relevant to, not in conflict with, responsible politics. According to him this is the best way one can serve his or her nation and religion at the same time without being fearful of God's and state's persecution. Gülen calls for a path of "right judgment, without going to extremes."[15]

In this context, Gülen reconciles Islam's worldly aspects with genuine democratic principles of governance:

> Religion focuses primarily on the immutable aspects of life and existence, whereas political, social, and economic systems or ideologies concern only certain variable social aspects of our worldly life....Likewise, worship and morality's universal and unchanging standards have little to do with time and worldly life.....religion has established immutable principles related to faith, worship and morality. Thus, only Islam's worldly aspects should be compared with democracy.[16]

FINDING A MIDDLE GROUND: THE CASE OF TURKEY

The reaction of many Muslims, in general, to secular democratic movements was either extremely hostile or reactive, particularly to the policies imposed on the population from the top ranks of the state mechanism. This is, in short, the history of state building in the Muslim world, at least for the last two centuries. In the face of the twin challenges of the ideological secularism and political Islamism Gülen has intended to reverse the ultra-secular course of history in Turkey through the peaceful means of mitigating ideological battles between the extreme secular establishment and religious forces. He was successful in persuading both sides that extremism of any kind is no answer to any crucial issues Turkey faces. Because of his religious background and his tolerant approach, the majority of people from all walks of life have accepted Gülen's ideas positively despite the concerted propaganda of a minority of hardline secularists who have tried to portray him as an enemy.

It is a profound belief in Islam that if you fail to respect people of other religions and race, then you are not even a Muslim in the true sense of the term. A renowned religious orthodox leader in Bangladesh named Hafezzi Huzur has propagated that "Muslims are our brethren in faith, while non-Muslims are our kin, since we are all children of Adam and Eve." Hafezzi Huzur's followers have failed to understand his teachings, while Gülen's articulation has caught the imagination of many millions of Turkish young men and women.

Gülen has spread this idea among the religious and secular circles of Turkey during the last four decades through his writings and preaching. Many wonder how he could find such a balanced path of preaching Islam in this age of hostility and intolerance. In fact, throughout Islamic history many Islamic scholars have tried to strike a balance between their passion to practice Islam wholeheartedly and their desire to show a deep-seated respect for other religions. Gülen has completely avoided all political and religious controversies, even at the height of his popularity at the turn of 21st century. He made it crystal clear that he has no intention of political involvement and that he does not support any political party.

Gülen has, however, proclaimed that Turkish politicians have no right to be corrupted or to deprive people from their due share in the democratic system and the social economic reforms the country urgently needs.

> As the Turkish people, we have accumulated many problems over the last several centuries. At their base lies our mistaken concentration on Islam's exterior and neglect of its inner pearl. Later on we began imitating others and surmised that there was a conflict between Islam and positive science....As ignorance is

the most serious problem, we must oppose it with education,
which always has been the most important way of serving our
country....Ignorance is defeated through education; poverty
through work and the possession of capital; and internal schism
and separation through unity, dialogue, and tolerance.[17]

Many so-called Islamic political parties have tried to claim a
bigger share in the political and economic affairs of their concerned
countries. In some countries, those who are labeled "Islamists"
were banned from politics or from participating in elections. In
other countries, military crackdowns have been used as a last resort
to stop these so-called Islamists from coming to the helm of state
power. For example, in 1992 Algeria was pushed to civil war to allow secularists to capture power illegally. Pakistani General Pervez
Musharraf was allowed to hold absolute power in the country for
about a decade (1999–2008) and went against all democratic
norms to serve the interests of other countries.

> The established democracies are accepting flawed and unfair
> elections for political expediency, Human Rights Watch said
> today [Washington, DC, January 31, 2008] in releasing its
> World Report 2008. By allowing autocrats to pose as demo-
> crats, without demanding they uphold the civil and political
> rights that make democracy meaningful, the United States, the
> European Union and other influential democracies risk under-
> mining human rights worldwide....It's now too easy for auto-
> crats to get away with mounting a sham democracy," said
> Kenneth Roth, executive director of Human Rights Watch....
> The United States and some allies have made it harder to
> demand other governments uphold human rights when they are
> committing abuses in the fight against terrorism. And when
> autocratic governments deflect criticism for violating human
> rights by pretending to be democrats, the global defense of
> rights is jeopardized, Human Rights Watch said.[18]

Within this global scenario, one could hardly imagine that in
ultra-secular Turkey the so-called Islamic forces would be able to
come to the power and retain it peacefully for a longer period of
time. The politicians with all their moderate character have proven

that they are capable of dealing with secular and nationalist forces of Turkey and of chairing the rapid development of economic growth. In 2007, Turkish exports reached 100 billion dollars for the first time. Turkey is now 17th largest economy in the world with a direct foreign investment exceeding 20 billion US dollars per year.[19]

Turkish secularists could not offer any rapid economic development by simply segregating religious people from non-religious people. Their divisive approach is "more like that of Descartes, who drew a red line between science and religion to prevent 'territorial violations.'"[20] Turkey was caught up with an internal cold war between religion and hard-line secularism that intensified with the heavy-handed interference and a strict headscarf ban in higher education institutions in 1997. Hard-line secularism did achieve a comparatively easy victory in holding governmental powers at all levels for some time and branded all kind of moderate Muslim political forces as Islamic fundamentalist forces. On the other hand, the governmental machine had become not only oppressive, but thoroughly corrupted.

Beginning in the late 1970's until the end of the 1980 Military Intervention, the Turkish economy was in a deep crisis for multiple reasons, including the spread of Marxist terror, political strife, poorly run government, and the growing disparity in economic classes. In that environment, Turkish moderate forces of all kinds began to create gradually an alliance against the corrupt elite after the restoration of civilian rule in 1984. The Turkish secular and ultra-nationalist elite did not take any steps toward even the possibility of the election of a government that would stand against religious freedom violations and remain neutral on religious issues.

With the collapse of the Soviet Union, atheism and secularism has lost its currency as a cross-border ideological exchange value for economic reforms. Thus the appeal of Islamic values has grown stronger to the masses as a remedy to the endemic corruption and horribly poor system of governance. Ultra-secular forces in Turkey wanted to block the so-called "Islamists" from power through elections. According to these forces, Turkey would not be allowed to go in any other direction other than the ultra-secularist way of development. For traditional Muslims, the ultra-secularists, who had been undermining the family values and Islamic culture up to the extent that the Turkish Muslim image was tarnished even in the neighboring Muslim countries, were already too much to bear.

The crisis of secularism has hardly been recognized in the West in recent decades. However, in his recent talk on "the Church and the challenge of secularization," Pope Benedict XVI said that secularism "invades all aspects of daily life and causes the development of a mentality in which God is effectively absent, entirely or in part, from human life and conscience. [This] is not just an external threat to believers, but has for some time been evident in the bosom of the Church herself."[21]

As an Islamic preacher of about four decades, Gülen was fully aware of how the interests of peaceful worshippers in numerous mosques in Turkey were in grave jeopardy for long time. However, he decided not to protest against the Turkish secular governments. Rather he continued his clarion call for calm and tranquility for all under all circumstances. Gülen has strongly supported moderation and compassion even in debates:

> Debate should not be for the sake of ego, but rather to enable the truth to appear. When we look at political debates in which the only thought is to vanquish the other person, there can be no positive result. For truth to emerge in a debate of ideas, such principles as mutual understanding, respect and dedication to justice cannot be ignored. As a Qur'anic rule debate can only take place in an environment that is conducive to dialogue....The great tyranny is to silence all the voices in one's conscience that express God. Tyranny also means committing an injustice against others, oppressing them and imposing one's ideas unto others. In that respect, as tyranny includes both polytheism and unbelief, it is the greater sin. Every polytheist or unbeliever may not be a wrongdoer in the sense outlined above. However, those who oppress others, who arm themselves in the name of committing evil, and who

> violate the rights of other people and the justice of God must
> be confronted within the framework of the law.[22]

In this statement we find a subtle difference between Gülen and his contemporary Muslim religious leaders, even many of his recent predecessors, who believe that first you have to change the state laws in line with Islamic principles and only then you can stop tyranny at the governmental levels and establish justice. Gülen alone argues that it is not at all wise to fight against your own tyrants violently, rather you need to try to change the framework of laws which might be very helpful in making the ruling elite understand that no one can so easily get away with violating people's legitimate rights. Playing an important role in formulating progressive public opinion, gradually the masses can keep both military and civil ruling systems under public pressure to achieve quite lofty goals for peace and justice for all. While Gülen was so determined and vigorous of his peaceful mission based on the Prophetic ideals of Islam, Pope Benedict XVI quoted unfortunately the anti-Islamic rhetoric of Byzantine Emperor Manuel II Paleologus: "Show me just what Muhammad brought that was new, and there you will find things only evil and inhuman, such as his command to spread by the sword the faith he preached." It is difficult for anybody to become appreciative of the role of a man like Prophet Muhammad, peace and blessings be upon him, in civilizing humankind if he or she thinks that brutal Byzantine Emperor Manuel II Paleologus is a right person to give fair evaluation about the Prophetic mission of spreading justice, love, peace, and a compassionate attitude to all.

As Ergene convincingly argues, the dissemination of false information as well as misconceptions created by different vested interest quarters are primarily responsible for giving harm to the peace-loving, pristine image of Islam:

> Betrayed by various media, it is impossible for the public to
> understand the political games that are being played in Algeria,
> Iran, Egypt, Afghanistan, Turkey, and Iraq. As long as they do
> not have access to sound knowledge and information about

Islam they will only be plunged into terror when faced with such images. The phenomenon of the rising Islamic awareness in the Muslim world today will be, for them, synonymous with international terrorism.[23]

While the West has often provided society with a biased image of Islam, often undermining the interests of the Muslim masses, Gülen has never even hinted at hostility toward any people or nations in any of his speeches or writing. Instead of just blaming people for their ignorance about Islam and Muslims, Gülen endeavors to convey the true message of Islam and to conduct interfaith dialogue between different religions and civilizations. Moreover, through his inter-faith dialogues, Gülen has demonstrated his utmost sincerity in trying to bring people of all faiths to the table of negotiation for the betterment of all of humankind and for the enlightenment of all human souls irrespective of race, religion, and gender.

CHAPTER 7

Gülen on *Jihad*, Tolerance, and Terrorism

GÜLEN ON *JIHAD*, TOLERANCE, AND TERRORISM

I n an era during which the media feeds the established anti-Islamic prejudice of many people, especially in the West, on front pages and news programs every day, *jihad* is guilefully equated with violence and terror. Emphasizing that *jihad* is "a command of God," Gülen elucidates two aspects of *jihad* in detail:

> *Jihad* takes place at two frontiers: inside and outside. A short definition for the former would be to strive to attain one's true being (greater *jihad*), whereas the latter is to help others in such an attainment (lesser *jihad*). The greater *jihad* is to overcome obstacles on the way to true being, reaching a knowledge of one's own self, thus attaining with further struggle the knowledge of God (*marifatu'llah*), love of God (*muhabbatu'llah*), and finally spiritual pleasure. The lesser *jihad*, on the other hand, aims to remove barriers between the faith and people, so that everyone is introduced to the knowledge of the Divine.[1]

Critical of the reductionist approach to *jihad*, which is mistakenly associated only with physical force, Gülen states that *jihad* is the effort to reach the point of being a perfected human being, and it embraces every kind of striving in God's cause and for the good of humanity. Gülen also reminds us that *jihad* does not mean using a sword:

> The lesser *jihad* is not a type of *jihad* only within the boundaries of a battlefield; this would be too limited a definition. Performing *jihad* may take place in a variety of ways and may range from even uttering of a word or keeping silent, grim face or a smile, leaving or joining a group, as long as each activity is done for God, and feelings like love and hatred are fine-tuned

in accordance with His pleasure. All struggles devoted to the reformation of a society, immediate family, relations, neighborhood, and town and in concentric circles all around the world are within the scope of lesser *jihad*.[2]

Pointing to the fact that the form of *jihad* has been different in different periods of time, he says:

> Just as sometimes counsel, sometimes guidance to another and sometimes taking a stand against unbelief are considered *jihad*, many times being a good example is also considered *jihad*. During the Age of Happiness for a certain time migration was considered equal to *jihad*... One youth who escaped and came to join a campaign was asked by the Prophet, "Do you have a mother or father who needs to be cared for?" When the answer was in the affirmative, the Prophet said, "Return home and make *jihad* for the sake of your unattended mother and father." By telling him to take care of them, the Prophet indicated that his *jihad* was taking care of his parents.[3]

Gülen states further "the fact that it is called 'lesser' *jihad* does not mean that it is insignificant; this is an expression which is simply out of comparison to the greater *jihad*."[4] He remarks that "the aim of either *jihad* is to purify believers of sin so that they may attain true humanity."[5] For Gülen, to become an ideal human being or Muslim is the real *jihad*. From all kinds of different Islamic perspectives, *jihad* is obviously an inner struggle to strive throughout the entire adult life to achieve higher degrees in *taqwa* (piousness) and to render services to the family, neighbors, and fellow-citizens in particular and the entire humankind in general. The scope of violence and terror in Islamic theology and thought is zero. Moreover, in resisting violence and aggression against innocent people and nations, the Qur'an has specified a number of strong principles to be followed by Muslims of all times. Indeed, "peace, not war, is essential in Islam, and war is a secondary situation resorted to in cases of defense, to stop tyranny, and when freedom of teaching of faith is violated."[6] God Almighty has indicated very clearly in the holy Qur'an that there would always remain some evil forces on earth that will try to destroy peace and harmony between peoples and religions:

> The believers against whom war is waged are given permission to fight in response, for they have been wronged. Surely, God has full power to help them to victory – those who have been driven from their homeland against all right, for no other reason than that they say, "Our Lord is God." Were it not for God's repelling some people by means of others, monasteries and churches and synagogues and mosques, where God is regularly worshipped and His Name is much mentioned, would surely have been pulled down (with the result that God is no longer worshipped and the earth becomes uninhabitable). God most certainly helps whoever helps His cause. Surely, God is All-Strong, All-Glorious with irresistible might. They are the believers who, if We give them authority on earth, without doubt establish the Prayer in conformity with its conditions, pay the Prescribed Purifying Alms fully, and enjoin and promote what is right and good and forbid and try to prevent the evil. With God rests the outcome for all matters. If they are denying you (O Messenger, you know that) before them the people of Noah, the Ad and the Thamud also denied (the Messengers sent to each.) And so too did the people of Abraham and the people of Lot; and the dwellers of Midian, and Moses too was denied (by the Pharaoh and his clan). Every time I granted respite to the unbelievers and then seized them (when they persisted in unbelief and injustices), how awesome was My disowning them! How many a township have We destroyed because it was given up to wrongdoing: so they all lie in ruins, with their roofs caved in, wells and fountains deserted, and towering, lofty castles collapsed. Do they never travel about the earth (and view all these scenes with an eye to learn lessons) so that they may have hearts with which to reason (and arrive at truth), or ears with which to hear (God's call)? For indeed it is not the eyes that have become blind, it is rather the hearts in the breasts that are blind. They challenge you to hasten the coming upon them of God's punishment (with which they are threatened). Let them know that God never fails to fulfill His promise; but a day with your Lord is like a thousand years in your reckoning. How many a township that was given up to wrongdoing have I given respite to, but then seized them

(when they persisted in unbelief and injustices); and to Me is the homecoming (Qur'an, 22:39–48).

It is very clear from the Qur'anic verses that *jihad* is not to destroy anything or anybody on earth, it is an utmost effort to uphold truth all the time against all odds. In other words, like any other theoretical and doctrinal issues in Islam, *jihad* had two different facets: material and spiritual. As Gülen notes,

> In a sense, the lesser *jihad* is material. The greater *jihad*, however, is conducted on the spiritual front, for it is our struggle with our inner world and carnal soul (*nafs*). When both of these *jihad*s have been carried out successfully, the desired balance is established. If one is missing, the other balance is destroyed.[7]

It is indeed a very serious and complicated issue to balance between material and spiritual aspects of *jihad* at the individual, national, and global level. The core issue is to sacrifice wealth, time, energy, and talent for the higher causes in life; i.e., for the sake of upholding truth, decency, humility, and human rights for all. To create such a phenomenon around us we all need to do a great deal of sacrifice for others. Each and every individual, the state, and agencies of all kinds those who have resources at their disposal have to be vigilant against the violation of any legitimate rights of others. The problem with the overwhelming majority of the Muslims is that they think they have very little resources left at their disposal to be spent for the causes of the God-Almighty; and as a result, many tiny groups in different parts of the world tend to believe that they have to make the ultimate sacrifice for their causes by putting their lives on the line. According to Gülen, however, real heroes are those who do not die but live for others. In this respect, sacrificing oneself for the service of others is an essential aspect of Gülen's teaching.

Unfortunately, we observe suicide attacks frequently employed as a tactical choice by different people or groups from different regions and religions of the world. As Karen Armstrong states, however, the terrorist act of such people or groups cannot be regarded as a Jewish, a Christian, or an Islamic act:

> Although Muslims, like Christians or Jews, have all too often failed to live up to their ideals, it is not because of the religion per se. We rarely, if ever, called the IRA bombings "Catholic" terrorism because we knew enough to realise that this was not essentially a religious campaign. Indeed, like the Irish republican movement, many fundamentalist movements worldwide are simply new forms of nationalism in a highly unorthodox religious guise. This is obviously the case with Zionist fundamentalism in Israel and the fervently patriotic Christian right in the US.[8]

Gülen states clearly that there is no any Islamic justification for taking lives unjustly, as attested in various Qur'anic verses:

> The Qur'an explicitly asserts that taking the life of one human being is the same as taking the lives of all of humanity: *"He who kills a soul unless it be (in legal punishment) for murder or for causing disorder and corruption on the earth will be as if he had killed all humankind; and he who saves a life will be as if he had saved the lives of all humankind"* (Maeda 5:32). It is impossible to see this much sensitivity on the issue of rights in any other religion or in modern law. Islam takes the issue so seriously as to equate the killing of one person with the killing of all of humanity....In another chapter, the Qur'an emphasizes that the eternal punishment of hell is the recompense for one who kills another unjustly: *"Whoever kills a believer intentionally, his recompense is Hell, to abide therein. And the wrath and the curse of God are upon him, and a dreadful penalty is prepared for him"* (Nisa 4:93). It should be noted that the word *halidan* in the verse is used by itself without the word *abadan*, or forever, being added. Although the word *abadan* is explicitly used in some other verses in the Qur'an, Ibn Abbas and some religious leaders of the generation that followed the Companions deduced from the word *halidan* being used in the verse that eternal punishment is the recompense of the murderer, the same as that for those who deny God.[9]

Gülen states that Islam, which means peace and justice in our individual and collective lives and is truly based on mercy and compassion, seeks to revive, not to kill. He emphasizes that an Islamic goal can be achieved only through Islamic means and methods. The means and methods employed can render one's political purposes religiously unjustified, as "neither Islam nor Muslims may be directed toward their real targets through diabolic means and methods."[10] Gülen publicly condemned the terrorist attack of 9/11 and refuted the association of Muslims with terrorism, calling upon everybody to condemn those who are darkening the bright face of Islam and to take collective action against them. Reminding us of the Islamic rule that one has no right to end one's own life, particularly to harm others, Gülen states:

> In Islam there are no suicide bombers. All throughout history Islam has never issued permission to murder innocent people; this is out of the question. However, as a consequence of the actions of some people, people similar to the Karmati and Kharijites, who have been deceived or manipulated by drugs or in some other way, many other innocents have been defamed, and pristine image of Islam has been tarnished. Muslims, the representatives of submission to God and security, have been depicted as potential terrorists.[11]

In an interview Gülen gave to *Zaman* daily's Nuriye Akman, Gülen further says:

> In Islam, killing a human is an act that is equal in gravity to unbelief. No one can touch an innocent person, even in the time of war. No one can give an Islamic legal pronouncement in this matter. No one can be a suicide bomber. No one can rush into crowds with bombs tied to his or her body. Regardless of the religion of these crowds, this is not religiously permissible.[12]

Thus the right question to be asked is not whether or not Islam allows or forbids suicide bombing or cruelty against declared enemy or adversaries, especially those who are so strong that one cannot fight them conventionally in any way. The core issue is that there are Muslims who have lost the compassionate soul that was supposed to take care of themselves and others around them. It did not happen overnight. It is a phenomenon that started much earlier than we can imagine or articulate fully for others. It might have started with religious disputes between different religions and races, but violence, war, and terrorism has intensified with the ideas that it is quite normal to use force to grab others' possessions or homeland without even asking any legal or moral question. Hippler's excellent analysis is worth-mentioning here:

> In the wars, massacres and other acts of political violence over the past one to two thousand years, there is no evidence of any differences in principle between the types of violence in different countries, regions or cultural groups. Waves of violence have never proceeded in a synchronized manner in all regions throughout history, occurring instead at different times and in different forms. Europe, Asia, America, Africa, Christian, Muslim, Hindu, Buddhists and other societies all have huge experience of political violence in the form of wars, mass murder, expulsion and repression...Whole books of Hebrew Bible are devoted to the military exploits of great kings, their contests relayed in gory details. The New Testament does not take up the battle cry immediately, but the later history of the church does, supplying a Christian record of bloody crusades and religious wars...There was conquest, tyranny and war in just about all societies and state systems, with the extent and form varying much more according to political contexts rather than cultural or religious aspects.[13]

During the entire colonial period and Cold War era the studies of the social sciences were in great confusion, and in fact, former colonists and big players in international politics are still engaged in brainwashing the youths of the Third and Muslim world countries. Religiously motivated scholars and authors are in most cases incapable of creating their own terms of reference to contemporary history, science, psychology, philosophy, and technology. Crisis in studying social and political sciences has become deepened in the wake of psychological warfare between the Muslim world and the

West. Both sides have often become reactive to the vital issues of human rights and human dignity. As Akhter notes,

> We are threatened by the engineering and industrialization of the life processes taking place in a global society where individualism and selfishness reign supreme, where profit making is the only morality of the civil society, where power and wealth is concentrated in a few hands and the world is divided sharply by rulers and the ruled, developed and underdeveloped, first and third or north and south, etc.[14]

Like many millions of us, Gülen has also been exposed to pressures and suppression of the government and its anti-people policies that have surrounded him in Turkey or elsewhere. However, he has never lost hope in persuading his people and others to come forward to undertake the role of peacemaker instead of spreading hatred and anger against other religions and even against his adversaries. Mark Scheel, a Western expert and analyst names Gülen as "Mahatma Gandhi of Turkey" and a "Modern Rumi" who has inspired the entire Turkish nation for peace and tranquility for all.[15]

In an interview Gülen says that lesser *jihad* "is undertaken only to remove obstacles before perfecting man morally and spiritually, and to bring about peace and order in human society."[16] Tolerance is important in bringing about peace within society. Emphasizing the importance of making *jihad* for tolerance, Gülen says that, "[s]ociety has to uphold tolerance. If we don't announce *jihad* for anything else, we should announce it for tolerance."[17]

HIZMET: GÜLEN'S WAY OF JIHAD

Gülen's writings and speeches are not confined in any particular area: he has written extensively on education, science and technology, psychology and philosophy, history, and economics. Moreover, he has always been very clear that the ultimate purpose of all his efforts is bringing people of different faith together. Through interfaith dialogue and multicultural education Gülen, has accomplished ground-breaking intellectual and spiritual work, the likes of which cannot be found in Muslim theology and polity in recent history. The Gülen movement has been popularly called *Hizmet*. In the literary sense *hizmet* means service, but in reality it is a communitarian imperative for all conscientious people to serve fellow citizens and others who happen to be around you. According to Gülen, education, for instance, is not only a religious obligation on both the individual and the community but also a sort of endless service (*hizmet*) to the students, society, and the world.

The universal vision Islam has propagated for many centuries was greatly harmed by many wars and conflicts. However, Muslim Sufis, jurists, and theologians have upheld many humane values inherited from Islamic civilization. Muslim scientists also transmitted the intellectual paradigms of research and the discovery of natural laws to the Westerners, who subsequently succeeded in using them for massive industrialization and urbanization. Becoming the victims of European colonialism and imperial exploitation and domination, many Muslims have lost Islamic hearts and souls dedicated to humanity at large and fellow citizens at home. Western and materialistic moral decadence has engulfed many Muslim nations in a way that they lost their political stability and intellectual integrity. Moreover, Muslim political and intellectual discourses were unable to have any real impact on the outcome of social studies as educational disciplines at institutional levels of schooling. Moreover, Muslim countries all over the world have begun to imitate destructive methods of acquiring scientific know-how and technology, destroying surrounding ecological and environmental systems.

> [I]n view of the West's chronic crisis in the aftermath of analytical deconstruction and the failure to reconstruct, it is incumbent upon Muslims armed with the epistemological methodology of the Qur'an to form close relations with the schools of Western analysis, whatever their trend or directions. These schools with the philosophical, intellectual and cultural bases are expanding day after day, and they provide a salubrious entry into epistemological methodology contact with the West for

the benefit of all humanity...The crisis of the West is a crisis of a deconstruction mode unable to reconstruct owing to the exclusion of the concepts of God, transcendence and revelation. The crisis in the Muslim world is manifested in the flawed methodology of dealing with a justifiable comprehensive heritage, one which is nevertheless, always encountered by a static mentality in interpreting that heritage, thus rendering it incapable of coming to terms with the concepts and methodologies of a contemporary and vibrant world.[18]

It is useless just to think that a country or people have grown into evil forces without any cause and effect relationship in the upbringing system of the youth. Overwhelming scientific success of the West automatically made the rest of the world subservient to the "White domination" over the vast majority of the world population. Racist South Africa under the domination of the White military power extended to many regions of the world. British India was just an invisible or misunderstood phenomenon of the same unjust and extremely cruel system of governance and exploitation that has no place in Islamic jurisprudence and theology. However, Muslims in a large number have failed to deal with the aftermath of colonial exploitation and the consequence of the nationalist movements leading to the fragmentation of the Muslim world into fifty-seven so-called independent Muslim countries.

The fundamental problem Muslim countries have faced is outdated educational systems and massive unemployment. All other problems, including social ills and economic fallouts from them are just the symptoms of the faulty educational, legislative, and judicial systems. Muslim nation-states still have not been able to make any headway in reforming any of the existing systems left behind by the colonial system and the Cold War rivalry between the USSR and the USA.

Involvement of Muslim nation-states in the "Great Power" politics in the international arena for many decades was either prompted from narrow-based partisan interests or dictatorial circles of extremely corrupted regimes of the Muslim countries. Thus

Muslim nations have lost the opportunities to build their own legal and political systems that could connect ruling elite to the grass-roots people in order to create a cohesive system of governance.

METAPHYSICAL LAWS OF NATURAL SCIENCES: LOST DIMENSIONS OF *JIHAD*

Islamic revealed knowledge by and large has an emphasis on the principles of metaphysical sciences that cannot be fully understood and realized merely by rules and regulations ingrained in the cosmic reality or dynamics. However, discoveries of scientific knowledge with its specificity and use of those scientific wonders in material life is rather quite helpful to understand the core essence of metaphysical sciences and the lessons from the divine ordinations. The understanding of the divinity in Islam is quite different from other conventional religious thoughts. No one can claim any divine connection to God-Almighty directly. However, like other "worlds of existence" humankind as a whole is definitely connected to the Transcendental divinity that governs the universe. The universe or any part of the cosmic world does not or cannot claim its full autonomy to run its systems in isolation.

A human being as an independent and lonely creature is indeed isolated materially but connected to its surroundings in every possible way. However, the humanness of its connection might be very limited, while heavenly connections have always remained diverse and complicated to the full comprehension of human *aql*, or the faculty of reason, which is more connected to the simple instinctual intellect rather than the greater horizons of wisdom and creditable methods of reaching higher degrees of intuitions without any prejudices and biases. Even the wisest or smartest intuitions cannot be regarded as *ilham*, or inspiration, to be treated as absolute truth about hidden or undiscovered phenomena or entities. It is nobody's job to declare who is higher than whom in the knowledge of *marifah*.[19]

In many Muslim countries and communities, there are many misconceptions about the avenues through which one can have an educational, experiential, and spiritual journey to achieve higher degrees of knowledge in *marifah*. Many religious superstitions are also manipulated in exercises related to *marifah* and many simple minded people are deceived by perverted clerics for their vested economic, political, and social interests. However, genuine spiritualists do exercise different methods of *marifah,* which is very helpful for enlightening any human soul or society. There is a widely-spread mistaken view about *marifah*, which is that *marifah* is an unscientific method of knowing truth about the material world and is rather an anti-thesis of scientifically established truth.

Gülen says that "[t]he opposite of (scientific) knowledge is ignorance, while the opposite of *marifah* is denial."[20] Denial to the fundamental truth in life and the hereafter has a serious consequence for individual citizens as well as for the entire society or nation at large. Such a denial of the ultimate truth that God-Almighty is the only source of absolute power and all other creatures are knowingly and unknowingly subordinate to the rules set forth from the same source, merciful and compassionate to all. Good deeds always lead to good consequences, and bad deeds only lead to bad consequences. This is like a scientific truth that can be proven in real material life at all levels, from the individual life to the lives of different nations. As Gülen puts it,

> A true concept of science will join spirituality and metaphysics with a comprehensive, inclusive view that affirms the intrinsic and unbreakable relation between any scientific discipline and existence as a whole. Only a concept embracing the whole in its wholeness can be called truly scientific. Seeing existence as discrete elements and trying to reach the whole from this will end up getting swamped in multiplicity. By contrast, embracing the whole and then studying its parts in the light of the whole allows us to reach sound conclusion about the reality of existence.[21]

In reality, it is not at all easy to balance or incorporate materialistic selfishness within a system in which the ruling elite and powerful segments voluntarily submit to the nobler and higher causes of humanity and safeguard the interests of the weaker sections of the population. Moreover, scientific know-how is rather easy to use in harmful ways, and misuse of advanced scientific knowledge can cause serious distress and agony in the poor, underprivileged, and destitute segments of population, who are incapable of paying the cost of modern facilities.

Any dramatic change in mode of production and distribution system of essential commodities in any state system demands serious scrutiny to protect the interest of the masses. In such cases, metaphysical knowledge or the imaginary power of human beings is even more valuable and powerful for the overall betterment of the society. Without imaginary power, human beings are just like other animals. Along with imaginary power, every human being needs to nurture his or her conscience with all kinds of humility (*tawadu*) toward others and well-regulated asceticism (*zuhd*) for the nourishment of body and soul. Here, not scientific knowledge, but the art of living and attachment to the right kinds of habits and avoidance of wrong kinds of habitual deeds serves the individual as well as society and state. Failing to provide such services to the causes of humanity, Muslims are surely bound to fail in all major religious and worldly affairs as well. On this topic, Gülen refers to the following Qur'anic verses:

> O you who have attained to faith! If you ever abandon your faith, God will in time bring forth [in your stead] people whom He loves and who love Him – humble towards the believers, proud towards all who deny the truth: [people] who strive hard in God's cause, and do not fear to be censured by anyone who might censure them: such is God's favor, which He grants unto whom He wills. And God is infinite, all-knowing.[22]

> For, [true] servants of the Most Glorious are [only] who walk gently on earth, and who, whenever the foolish address them, reply with [words of] peace.[23]

The style of Muslim way of living and thinking, *muraqaba* (contemplation with strong self regulation), occupies a very important role in finding the right place for a Muslim to live and work. Without that spiritual or metaphysical component of the Muslim life-style at personal level, any Muslim could join any violent group to bring about a dramatic change in the economic, political, and social environment in which he or she lives. As Islam entertains no belief for clergymen to act as mediators between human beings and God, Muslims have to understand and incorporate into their lives the practice of *muraqaba*, or self-supervision, that helps Muslim men and women sustain peace and creativity throughout their entire lives. Gülen pays a special attention to this concept: "*Muraqaba* is one of the most important and direct ways of reaching God without a guide. It resembles the type of sainthood attained through succession to the Prophetic mission, which is conveying the Divine Message to people, without following a spiritual order."[24]

Possibly no other religion on earth would allow you to try to reach a universal God's blessing directly without any agent or middleman between the human being and the ultimate Creator. While Islam does not admit any system of priesthood, or sacerdotalism, still a spiritual mentor or guide can help the initiates travel safely on the Straight Path and therefore prevent them from suffering from any diversions from the path in their journey toward God.

The feeling of *fana* (the diminishing of the ego in the light of God) and the concept of *insan al-kamil* (man or woman who lives by the explicit and implicit rules of God) as a psychological stage or mental condition may lead some individual Muslims to go astray, especially when they have no religious or spiritual guidance. In the absence of a living religious and spiritual guide, one may receive help directly from the scientific discoveries available to be used for the benefits of society or state at large and people living in distressful conditions, in particular. However, the most difficult task is how to correlate metaphysical thoughts with concrete scientific knowledge, which has its own limitations and boundaries. Gülen notes the following:

> Remember that the most important source of science, thinking, and art, virtues and morality, is metaphysics. All of existence can be perceived with a sound mode of thinking based on pure metaphysics. This allows us to view all of existence as a whole and to travel through its deeper dimensions. Without spirituality and metaphysics, we cannot build a community on sound foundations; such communities are forced to beg continuously from others. Communities that lack some metaphysical concepts suffer from identity crisis.[25]

Without a doubt we can now conclude that along with many other peoples, many Muslim nations and ethnicities have been suffering from serious identity crises. This is not a national or sectarian identity problem. A Muslim can easily claim that he or she is Shi'i or Sunni and Hanafi, Shafi'i, Maliki or Hanbali within Sunni Islam. However, in real spiritual terms or in terms of living a life of humility, these differences mean very little and are simply differences in ritualistic practices. Many rituals are definitely an integral part of Islamic spiritual way of living, but none of those rituals alone can automatically bring benefit to any practitioner of any sect or religion if they are not followed by concrete material benefits to the concerned people and their societies.

What we can observe today all over the world is that the richer we get as states or nations, the sufferings of the poorer segments of all societies increases with an unbearable and horrible speed. The gap between the rich and the poor increases every day and every moment with alarming consequences, including making people completely hopeless and helpless with no food, drinking water, decent shelter, morally sound education, and medicine for even simple curable diseases. Some people were driven out from their ancestors' homes forever similar to a total ethnic cleansing and have nowhere to take refuge as dignified normal human beings, who are supposed to take care of their families successfully so that their mission on earth as spiritual and physical entities would be meaningful and distinct from other creatures.

The whole discourse about Islamic identity and Muslim culture is now in the wrong hands or in a faulty state machinery across the board. And this crisis began much earlier than we can fully comprehend. Colonial oppression of Muslim men and women is just one aspect of an expansive and complicated identity crisis that is going on in the Muslim world in full swing. According to Katherine Bullock,

> "This is because of the nineteenth century discourse on the hierarchy of civilizations and the belief of the Europeans in their own superiority and in the necessity of their quest for the Middle East. The status of women became the benchmark of the rank a civilization had in the hierarchy. Islam was placed below Christianity (with Eastern Christianity itself placed below Latin Christianity), but above pagan Africa and the native peoples of the colonies (North America/Canada/Australia)... They [Muslim women] are slaves to their husbands, and allowed to see no other persons at home than their families or relations, and when they do appear in the streets, their faces are completely veiled.... [T]he European notion of the harem was already an idea predicated on the ages-old Orientalist fantasy of the exotic Middle East...This harem fantasy drew on the Middle Ages Christian polemic against Islam that was revived in the nineteenth century. Islam was supposedly an overly indulgent religion that scandalously allowed divorce, remarriage, and polygamy. For Christians, medieval and modern, this was proof of Islam's status as false religion."[26]

With the colonial mind and ultra-secular indoctrination, some people even from the countries whose population is predominantly Muslim now believe that Islam is really a false religion and that Christianity is superior to so-called Eastern religions. As a defense, many Muslim scholars and devout Muslims claim that Islam is not at all a religion in any conventional way as Europeans or Westerners understand. Instead, Islam is a *Din*[27], i.e. a way of living, thinking, and working according to the will of God based on the revealed and acquired knowledge demonstrated through wisdom of the prophetic lifestyle. Absence of such a lifestyle as a mainstream practice in any society or state ultimately leads the younger generation to violence, which has nothing to do with any of the fundamentals of Islam.

GÜLEN'S RESPONSE TO THE CLASH OF CIVILIZATIONS THESIS

According to Gülen, "those who are looking forward to a catastrophic future for the world and a clash of civilizations are individuals or groups who are unable to impose their world view on the people and hope that global antagonisms will ensure the continuation of their power in the world.[28]

Unfortunately many such misguided groups of politicians and statesmen across the board name all kinds of violent and terrorist acts as *jihad* and call devout and peace loving Muslims "Islamists," "jihadists," or "fundamentalist." One of the reasons why the West could use that propaganda against Islam is that it maintains the upper hand in technology and media. The monopoly many Westerners now have over the use of high technology for destructive purposes is a dangerous situation for the existence and survival of the entire world. Instead of fighting that danger using violent ways and means, Gülen has tried to mitigate that dispute through dialogue. Gülen has rejected the idea of "the clash of civilizations" concocted in the Western academia and media. However, many believe that this concept of a clash of civilizations in the West was prompted by the religious ideas about the original emergence of human beings on earth. Let's look at Bullock's comparative analysis:

> So, to emphasize, in Islam there is nothing evil or undesirable about the body and its desires. Woman, although partaking in the Fall, is not held responsible for the expulsion from paradise (Adam is). There is no original sin [in Islam]...It is also worth pointing out that unlike Christianity, which enshrines the masculine principle in the image of 'God the father' and Jesus the 'Son of God' or goddess religions that sanctify the feminine principle in the image of the Divine, in Islam, neither masculine nor feminine principle is enshrined in the Divine. God is neither the father, nor the Mother, nor the son.[29]

This is the foundation of the discord between Muslims and Christians over religious and civilizational issues. However, many

Christian sects, such as the Universal Unitarian Church, Quakers, and many other groups, have come out from these narrow-based conflicts with the Muslims. Like many orthodox Christians, many reactionary Muslims are also being caught with this never ending ideological fight over civilizational issues. However, in reality, fighting over civilizational issues has taken the shape of military brutality of stronger powers over smaller and weaker nations. The Islamic approach to politics and economics has always been against such uneven wars and extreme brutality. This is the reason many name Islam as a "religion of harmony, peace, and justice." Though the concept of the *din al-fitra*[30] is much broader than that, God clearly warned Muslims to be very cautious in word and deed, especially when it comes to war or violence:

> My Mercy embraces all things; and so, (although in the world every being has a share in My Mercy, in the Hereafter) I will ordain it for those who act in reverence for Me and piety and pay their Prescribed Purifying Alms, and they are those who truly believe in all of Our Revelations and signs... He enjoins upon them what is right and good and forbids them what is evil; he makes pure, wholesome things lawful for them, and bad, corrupt things unlawful. And he relieves them of their burdens and the restraints that were upon them...[31]

For a long time, especially from the eighth century to the Renaissance when the Muslim world was the most advanced and powerful in the world, Muslims contributed substantially in all fields of science and technology and even cooperated with their adversaries and enemies in spreading ethically sound educational avenues to open the doors of mysteries implanted and infused in the Book of Universe. However, using scientific knowledge for the betterment of the whole humankind or educating others, the Muslim ruling elite in many cases were forgetful in regards to their responsibilities to their own people. Otherwise, the knowledge and experience Muslims handed over to the West would not have been so easily used against the Muslim and Islamic interests. Hearing such an argument, many Westerners today laugh at the Muslims' claim that Muslim scientists had created the foundation of modern science upon which the modern technological world was built.

> Their [Muslims'] victory in Western China in the eight century enabled the Muslims to benefit from contemporary Chinese technologies, such as paper making, which they in turn introduced into the entire Muslim world including [Andalusian] Spain. From there it was taken to the rest of the Europe. This indeed was a revolutionary discovery leading to the wider dissemination of knowledge and democratization of learning.[32]

The thread of dissemination of knowledge from Muslim nations to the rest of the world, in one way or another, continued for about one thousand years until the recent colonial domination over the Muslim nations. The horrible consequences of colonial domination over Muslim nations were brought by the newly discovered destructive methods of international politics, diplomacy, and technology. Fearing Western unethical educational systems under extreme secular or anti-religious policies, many Muslim nations tried to hinder the spread of modern scientific know-how and technology in their countries as a way of safeguarding them from Western moral decadence.[33]

Scientific knowledge and technology has been made free from all obligations to the universal ethical and moral values. Western imperial powers could not possibly wage two world wars within the first half of the twentieth century without the technological capabilities they had at their disposal. Since then the brutality has continued throughout the Muslim populated nations and Third World countries. In today's globalized world where we are connected easily, unlike any other period in history, the best hope for humankind is to embrace a world of peace and understanding where aggressions of power is discouraged while dialogue of civilizations is fostered. Hopefully, Muslim nations as whole will emerge as a powerful force to deter all kinds of terrorist acts all over the world. And hopefully, Western powers will also come forward to stop all aggressive wars against smaller nations. Only then will Gülen's ideals be heard loudly in every corner of the world.

In the name of Allah,

the All-Merciful, the All-Compassionate.

Allah! There is no god but He, the Living, the Self-subsisting,

Eternal. No slumber can seize Him nor sleep.

His are all things in the heavens and on earth.

Who is there that can intercede in His presence except as He permits?

He knows what (appears to His creatures as) before or after or

behind them. Nor shall they compass any of His knowledge except as

He wills. His Throne does extend over the heavens and the earth, and

He feels no fatigue in guarding and preserving them for He is the

All-High, the Supreme in glory.

NOTES

Introduction

1 Mark Scheel, "A Communitarian Imperative: Fethullah Gülen's Model of Modern Turkey," *The Fountain*, Issue 61, January–February 2008.

2 Gurkan Celik, Kate Kirk and Yusuf Alan, "Gülen's Definition of Peace," *Dialogue: Asia-Pacific*, Issue 15, January–March 2008, p. 8.

3 M. Fethullah Gülen, *Toward a Global Civilization of Love and Tolerance*, New Jersey: The Light, 2006, pp. 6, 8, 59.

4 Şükran Vahide, "Bediüzzaman Said Nursi's Official Biography," http://www.witness-pioneer.org/vil/Books/SV_Nursi/Conclusion.htm.

5 http://www.foreignpolicy.com/story/cms.php?story_id=4408.

Chapter 1: Gülen Echoes Rumi with a Difference

1 M. Fethullah Gülen, *The Statue of Our Souls: Revival of Islamic Thought and Activism*, New Jersey: The Light, 2007, p. 91.

2 Turgut Özal (1927–1993) founded the Motherland Political Party (ANAP) and was elected as its leader on May 20, 1983. His party won the elections, and he formed the government and became the Prime Minister. After his premiership, which ran from December 1983 and November 1989, he became the President and died in 1993 of a sudden heart attack while he was still on duty.

3 M. Fethullah Gülen, *The Statue of Our Souls: Revival of Islamic Thought and Activism*, New Jersey: The Light, 2007, pp. 36–37.

4 Ibid., p. 34.

5 Here the term "Islamic" means anything honest and sincere that is dedicated to the cause of humanity and the welfare of any people or even any creature on Earth or in Heaven.

6 Ihsan Yilmaz, "Rumi's Renewed Social Innovation and Pluralist Activism Today," International Mevlana Jalaluddin-i Rumi Conference, Dushanbe, September 7, 2007.

7 "The West Has Tried to Hide Mevlana's Relation with Islam" In: http://en.fGülen.com/content/view/2321/22/.

8 Elisabeth Özdalga, "Worldly Asceticism in Islamic Casting: Fethullah Gülen's inspired piety and activism," *Critique*, Issue 17, Fall, 2003, pp. 83–104.

9   Joshua D. Hendrick, "The Regulated Potential of Kinetic Islam: Antitheses in Global Islamic Activism," *Muslim Citizens of the Globalized World*. Robert A. Hunt, Yuksel A. Aslandogan (eds.), New Jersey: The Light, 2007, pp. 28–29.

10 Seema Arif, "The Memetic Counseling of Masnavi: The Artless Art of Jalaladdin Rumi," *Rumi and His Sufi Path of Love*. M. Fatih Citlak and Huseyin Bingul (eds.), New Jersey: The Light, 2007, p. 31.

11 M. Dinorshoyev, "Foreword," *The Dghemchudghini [Jewels] of Jalaluddin Balkhi: Masnavi, Izbrannoe Raskazi I Pritchi*, Dushanbe, 2007, pp. 14–15.

12 In the literature, the term *ummi* Islam refers to popular Islam, which cannot be destroyed. Neither the Soviet regimes in the Central Asian countries nor the secular regimes of Arabs or Turks ultimately succeeded in overcoming popular Islam that lives in the hearts and minds of the common people or ordinary masses.

13 Mahatma Gandhi, quoted in Easwaran, Ekrath, *Nonviolent Soldier of Islam: Badshah Khan, A Man to Match His Mountains*, Nilgiri Press, 1999.

14 M. Dinorshoyev, "Foreword," *The Dghemchudghini [Jewels] of Jalaluddin Balkhi: Masnavi, Izbrannoe Raskazi I Pritchi*, Dushanbe, 2007, pp. 16–17.

15 See Ali Bulac, "The Most Recent Reviver in the Ulama Tradition: The Intellectual Alim, Fethullah Gülen,"*Muslim Citizens of the Globalized World*, Robert A. Hunt, Yuksel A. Aslandogan (eds.), New Jersey: The Light, 2007, p. 118.

16 Ibid.

CHAPTER 2: SUFISM IN THEORY AND PRACTICE: GÜLEN'S PERSPECTIVE

1   M. Fethullah Gülen, *Toward a Global Civilization of Love and Tolerance*, New Jersey: The Light, 2006, p. 166.

2   Rumi, *Divan-i Kabir*, from Ghazal no: 563.

3   M. Fethullah Gülen, *Key Concepts in the Practice of Sufism: Emerald Hills of the Heart*, Vol. 3, New Jersey: Tughra Books, 2009, p. 270.

4   Ibid., pp. 39–40, 37–56.

5   Ibid., Vol. 1, New Jersey: The Light, 2006 , p. xix.

6   http://en.mfethullahgulen.net/press-room/claims-and-answers/1216-claims-and-answers.html

7   Ali Ünal, "Foreword," *Key Concepts in the Practice of Sufism: Emerald Hills of the Heart*, Vol. 3, M. Fethullah Gülen, New Jersey: Tughra Books, 2009, p. ix.

8   Gülen, *Key Concepts in the Practice of Sufism*, Vol. 3, p. x.

9   Ibid., Vol. 3, p. xii.

10   Ibid., Vol. 2, p. xvii.

11   Ibid., Vol. 2, p. xix.

12   Ibid, p. xii.

13   Ibid.

14   A *mujtahid* may lead any group of Muslims in finding appropriate solutions to the problems at hand in his community and beyond.

15   Gülen, ibid., Vol. 2, p. xxi.

16   Ibid., Vol. 2, p. xxiii.

17   Qur'an, 16: 125.

18   Gülen, ibid., Vol 2, p. 26.

19   Ibid., Vol 2, pp. 26–27.

20   See A.B.M. Mahbubul Islam, *Islamic Constitution: Qur'anic & Sunnatic Perspective*, Dhaka: Professors Publication.

21   Gordon R. Woodman, "Globalization, Social and Religious Diversity, Legal Pluralism: Can State Law Survive?," *Law Journal*, issue 15:2, 2007, pp. 159, 161.

22   Gülen, ibid., Vol 2, p. 152.

23   Gülen, ibid., p. xvi.

24   http://www.fethullahGülen.org/content/view/857/50/

25   This universal ethical law appears in the Qur'an five times. See also 17:15; 35: 18, 39: 7; 53: 38.

26   Here stupor means a state of mind with passionate love for God and heavenly systems or Divine gifts and manifestations that surround us all.

27   Gülen, ibid., Vol, 2, pp. 39, 41.

28   Gülen, *The Statue of Our Souls: Revival in Islamic Thought and Activism*, New Jersey: The Light, 2007, p. 22. For the details on the issue, see Gülen's concept of "the Inheritors of the Earth" in the same work, pp. 31–42.

29   Gülen, *Questions and Answers About Islam*, Vol. 2, New Jersey: The Light, 2005, pp. 22–23.

30   Abdun Noor, *Social Justice and Human Development*. Dhaka: Adorn Publication, 2007, p. 95.

31   Gülen, *Key Concepts in the Practice of Sufism*, Vol 2, p. 223.

32   Ibid., p. 209.

33   Ibid., Vol 1, p. 7.

34   Gülen, *Questions and Answers about Islam*, Vol., 2, New Jersey: The Light, 2005, p. 23.

35   Gülen, *Key Concepts in the Practice of Sufism*, Vol. 1, p. 30.

36   Qur'an, 48: 10, 14.

37 Qur'an, 14: 5-6.
38 Gülen, *Key Concepts in the Practice of Sufism*, Vol. 1, pp. 79, 86–87.
39 Very recently it has been established by science that there are independent solar systems more than fifteen thousand light years away from the solar system we live in.
40 A. Kadir Yildirim, "Islam and Democracy: A Critical Perspective on a Misconstrued Relationship," *The Fountain*, Issue 61, January–February, 2008, p. 15.

CHAPTER 3: GÜLEN'S METHODOLOGY OF SCHOOLING:
EDUCATIONAL ENLIGHTENMENT AT HOME AND ABROAD

1 Gülen, "An Interview with Gülen," *The Muslim World*, Hartford, Vol. 95, Number 3, July 2005, p. 451.
2 The Ottoman sultanate was formally abolished in 1923. The collapse of the Ottoman sultanate was not unaccepted. However, no Muslim nations, including Arab nations, gained anything substantial out of the demise of the Ottoman state as a political center for the entire *umma*. See Fred H. Lawson, Constructing International Relations in the Arab World. Stanford, 2006. pp. 1–14.
3 Jill Irvine, "The Gülen Movement and Turkish Integration in Germany," *Muslim Citizens of the Globalized World*. Robert A. Hunt and Yuksel A. Aslandogan (eds.), New Jersey: The Light, 2007, p. 64.
4 Yuksel A. Aslandogan and Muhammed Cetin, "Gülen's Educational Paradigm in Thought and Practice,"*Muslim Citizens of the Globalized World*. Robert A. Hunt and Yuksel A. Aslandogan (eds.), New Jersey: The Light, 2007, pp. 34–35.
5 The strictly regulated religious education in Turkey has a close similarity with the management of religious education in the Central Asian Soviet republics under communism. According to the Turkish constitution: Education and instruction in religion and ethics shall be conducted under State supervision and control. (Article 24/4.)
6 Ihsan Yilmaz, "State, Law, Civil Society and Islam in Contemporary Turkey," *The Muslim World*, Hartford, Vol. 95, Number 3, July 2005.
7 On March 12, 1971 Fethullah Gülen was arrested under a mere suspicion that he might have some connection with some subversive activities against the government. However, after six months he was found completely innocent and was released by a court order and resumed his official job as a modern clergy to preach the Islamic faith and spirituality to his own audience.

8   Ihsan Yilmaz, "State, Law, Civil Society and Islam in contemporary Turkey," *The Muslim World*, Hartford, Vol. 95, Number 3, July 2005, p. 399.

9   Yuksel A. Aslandogan and Muhammed Cetin, "Gülen's Educational Paradigm in Thought and Practice,"*Muslim Citizens of the Globalized World*, Robert A. Hunt and Yuksel A. Aslandogan (eds.), New Jersey: The Light, 2007, p. 35.

10   Ibid.

11   Sir Syed Ahmed, Mawlana Abul Kalam Azad and Ali Brothers are only few names in the long list of people pursuing a path of accommodation between religious and modern education.

12   Lester R. Kurtz, "Gülen's Paradox: Combining Commitment and Tolerance," *The Muslim World*, Hartford, Vol. 95, Number 3, July 2005, pp. 380–381.

13   Gülen, *Advocate of Dialogue*, compiled by Ali Unal and Alphonse Williams. Virginia: The Fountain, 2000, p.151.

14   Ibid.

15   "In 1096 the first Crusade began its eastward march; in 1098 the great cities of Edessa and Antioch and many fortresses were taken; in 1099 the Christians regained possession of Jerusalem itself. In the next few years the greater part of Palestine and the coast of Syria, Tortosa, Akka, Tripolis, and Sidon (1110) fell into the hands of the Crusaders, and the conquest of Tyre in 1124 marked the apogee of their power. It was the precise moment when a successful invasion from Europe was possible. A generation earlier, the Seljuk power was inexpugnable. A generation later, a Zengi or a Nureddin, firmly established in the Syrian seats of the Seljuk Turks, would probably have driven the invaders into the sea. A lucky star led the preach-ers of the first Crusade to seize an opportunity of which they hardly real-ized the significance. Peter, the Hermit and Urban II chose the auspicious moment with sagacity as- unerring as- if they had made a profound study of Asiatic politics. The Crusade penetrated like a wedge between the old wood and the new, and for a while seemed to cleave the trunk of Mohammadan Empire into splinters" (Stanley Lane-Poole, *History of Egypt in the Middle Ages*, 1968:163–164).

16   Imam Khomeini, *Prablenie Fakixa: Islamskoe Problenie*, Tehran: Institute of Learning and Publication of the Works of Imam Khomeini, 2003, pp. 29-30.

17   Gülen, "Foreword," *Advocate of Dialogue*, compiled by Ali Unal and Alphonse Williams. Virginia: The Fountain, 2000, p. v.

18 The Indian sub-continent is a place where **40%** of the total Muslim population lives, and it still maintains a very rich legacy of Islamic heritage and Muslim culture.

19 See Conn Hallinan, "Politics By Other Means: Religion and Foreign Policy," *Counterpunch*, Issue 2, October, 2007, http://www.counterpunch.org/hallinan10022007.html.

20 In the oil rich Arab world, one in five Arabs still live on less than $2 a day. This is not an isolated phenomenon. Over the past 20 years, growth in income per head, at an annual rate of 0.5%, was lower than anywhere else in the world except sub-Saharan Africa. After so much talk about economic growth and development in Pakistan, 40% of the land is in the hands of 23 families. This is no more a Muslim phenomenon; it is an endemic economic disaster of catastrophic scale over the entire planet where 1.3 billion people live on less than one dollar a day and another 3 billion live on fewer than two dollars a day. From amongst them 1.3 billion have no access to clean water, 3 billion have no access to sanitation, and 2 billion have no access to electricity. On the other hand, a few thousand billionaires have been controlling the world economy and dictating most of the governments to destroy the entire ecological and environmental system world-wide for their vested financial interests. See, http://www.economist.com/displaystory.cfm?story_id=121339222

21 M. Fethullah Gülen, *The Statue of our Souls: Revival of Islamic Thought and Activism*, New Jersey: The Light, 2007, pp. 54, 55.

22 B. Jill Carroll, *A Dialogue of Civilizations: Gülen's Islamic Ideals and Humanistic Discourse*, New Jersey: The Light, 2007, p. 77.

23 Gülen, *The Statue of our Souls*, p. 154.

24 About 20% of its over 70 million Turkish population live in poverty even though it is a world leader in agricultural production. Since March 2007, Turkey is the world's largest producer of hazelnuts, figs, apricots, cherries, quince, and pomegranates; the second largest producer of watermelons, cucumbers, and chickpeas; the third largest producer of tomatoes, eggplants, green peppers, and lentils; the fourth largest producer of onions and olives; the fifth largest producer of sugar beets; the sixth largest producer of tobacco, tea, and apples; the seventh largest producer of cotton and barley; the eighth largest producer of almonds; the ninth largest producer of wheat, rye, and grapefruits; and the tenth largest producer of lemons. See, http://ntvmsnbc.com/news/403824.asp

25 Carroll, p. 99.

26 Gülen, *Advocate of Dialogue,* p. 244.

Chapter 4: Gülen's Approach to the Qur'an and Ideal Society

1 Gülen, *Toward a Global Civilization of Love and Tolerance*, pp. 146-147.

2 Asma Barlas, *"Believing Women" in Islam: Unreading Patriarchal Interpretations of the Qur'an*, University of Texas Press, 2002, pp. 21–22.

3 Gülen, *Questions and Answers about Islam*, Vol. 1, pp. 81–82.

4 H. Patrick Glenn, *Legal Traditions of the World*, 2000, pp. 173–74.

5 *Abu Dawud*, "Diyat," 70; *Tirmidhi*, "Diyat," 17.

6 *Ibn Hanbal*, 411.

7 Gülen, *The Messenger of God, An Analysis of the Prophet's Life*, New Jersey: The Light, 2005, p. 152.

8 Bernard Lewis, *What Went Wrong? Western Impact and Middle Eastern Response*, NY: Oxford University Press, 2002.

9 M. Ahsan Khan, *Human Rights in the Muslim World: Fundamentalism, Constitutionalism, and International Politics*, Carolina Academic Press, 2003, p. 110.

10 Qur'an, 5:38.

11 H. Patrick Glenn, *Legal Traditions of the World*, 2000, pp. 170–71.

12 Noah Feldman, *The Fall and Rise of the Islamic State*, New Jersey: Princeton University Press, 2008.

13 Gülen, *Toward A Global Civilization of Love and Tolerance*, p. 186.

14 Ibid.

15 These are the four Sunni schools of law: Hanafi, Maliki, Shafi'i, and Hanbali as well as one major Shi'i school.

16 http://www.fethullahGülenGülen.org/content/view/2854/3/

17 "An Interview with Fethullah Gülen," *The Muslim World*, Hartford, Vol. 95, Number 3, July 2005p. 454.

18 Asma Barlas, "Believing Women" in *Islam: Unreading Patriarchal Interpretations of the Qur'an*, p. 9.

19 Saadedine El `Othmani, "Islam and Civil State," In: http://www.islamon-line.net/English/contemporary/2005/10/article03.shtml#1

20 "Understanding Saudi Islam-Wahhabism," In: http://www.freemuslims.org/document.php?id=38

21 Gülen, *Toward a Global Civilization of Love and Tolerance*, p. 230.

22 Richard Henry Drummond, *Islam for the Western Mind: Understanding Muhammad and the Qur'an*, Hampton Roads Publishing Co., 2005, p. 62.

23 See Dominique Sourdel, *Medieval Islam*, London: Routledge, 1979, pp. 59–61.

24 The foundation of the Islamic faith depends on the belief that the Prophet Muhammad, peace and blessings be upon him, received the incorruptible words of God as the final Revelation to the entire human race in order to spread a comprehensive version of spiritual and mundane salvation for all men and women.

25 M. Fethullah Gülen, *Questions & Answers about Islam*, Vol., 1, pp. 90–91.

26 "An Interview with Fethullah Gülen," *The Muslim World*, Hartford, Vol. 95, Number 3, July 2005, pp. 455-6.

27 *The Message of the Qur'an*, Complete Edition, Translated and Explained by Muhammad Asad , Gibraltar: Dar Al-Andalus, 1980, p. 270.

28 Ali Ünal, *The Qur'an with Annotated Interpretation in Modern English*, New Jersey: The Light, 2006, p. 380.

29 David Brooks, "Trading Cricket for Jihad," *The New York Times*, (August 4, 2005; http://www.nytimes.com/2005/08/04/opinion/04brooks.html?t h=&emc=th&pagewanted=print

30 Secularism as a democratic principle in the West means that religious and state affairs function independently for the uninterrupted development of both aspects of same society, while secularism has been used in many Muslim countries as a tool of suppression of popular voice against exploitative government machinery. Thus Muslim secularists are equally condemned in many Muslim countries as their fanatic religious counterparts. Extremism as a phenomenon is almost equally shared by many Muslim secularists and Islamists with no profound spiritual footing.

31 Gülen, "On the Holy Qur'an and Its Interpretation,"in his foreword to *The Qur'an with Annotated Interpretation of the Qur'an in Modern English*. New Jersey: The Light, 2006.

Chapter 5: Gülen's Notion of *Hizmet* and Public Good: From a Strategy to an Action Plan

1 Bekim Agai, "The Gülen Movement's Islamic Ethics of Education," *Turkish Islam and the Secular State: The Gülen Movement*. M. Hakan Yavuz and John L. Esposito (eds.), New York: Syracuse University Press, 2003, p. 59.

2 Zeki Saritoprak, "Fethullah Gülen: A Sufi in his Own Way," *Turkish Islam and the Secular State: The Gülen Movement*, p. 167.

3 Ibid., p. 159.

4 Ibid., p. 169.

5 M. Hakan Yavuz, "The Gülen Movement: The Turkish Puritans," *Turkish Islam and the Secular State: The Gülen Movement*, pp. 26–27.

6   In the many dimensions of his lifetime of achievement, as well as in his personality and character, Bediüzzaman Said Nursi was and, through his continuing influence, still is an important thinker and writer in the Muslim world. Nursi was not a writer in the usual sense of the word. He wrote his splendid work the *Risale-i Nur*, a modern commentary of the Qur'an exceeding 5,000 pages, because he had a mission: he struggled against the materialistic and atheistic trends of thought fed by science and philosophy and tried to present the truths of Islam to modern minds and hearts of every level of understanding. Quoted from "Bediüzzaman and the Risale-i Nur," *Humanity's Encounter with the Divine Series*, New Jersey, Tughra Books, 2009.

7   M. Hakan Yavuz, "Islam in the Public Sphere: The Case of the Nur Movement," *Turkish Islam and the Secular State: The Gülen Movement*, pp. 17–18.

8   Yavuz, "The Gülen Movement: The Turkish Puritans," *Turkish Islam and the Secular State: The Gülen Movement*, p.19.

9   Ahmet T. Kuru, "Fethullah Gülen's Search for a Middle Way: Between Modernity and Muslim Tradition," *Turkish Islam and the Secular State: The Gülen Movement*, p. 123.

10 Mehmet Enes Ergene, *An Analysis of the Gülen Movement: Tradition Witnessing the Modern Age*, New Jersey: Tughra Books, 2008, pp. 16–17.

11 See Nevval Sevindi, *Contemporary Islamic Conversations: Fethullah Gülen on Turkey, Islam and the West*, Albany: State University of New York Press, 2008, pp. 71–79; Etga Ugur, "Intellectual Roots of 'Turkish Islam' and Approaches to the 'Turkish Model,'" *Journal of Muslim Minority Affairs*, Vol. 24, October, 2004, pp. 327–346.

12 Ergene, pp. 12–13, 20

13 Cited in Ergene, p. 115.

CHAPTER 6: GÜLEN'S THOUGHTS ON MODERN DEMOCRACY

1   Editor's note: Khawarij or Kharijites ("seceders," or literally "those who went out") are the earliest sect to advocate a fundamentalist outlook of Islam. During the caliphate of Ali, the Khawarij separated themselves from mainstream Islam, and one of them assassinated the righteous Caliph in 661. They were a reactionary group who set about creating an ideal society through violence.

2   Hulusi Turgut, "Nurculuk," *Sabah daily*, January 23–31, 1997.

3   "An Interview with Fethullah Gülen," *The Muslim World*, Hartford, Vol. 95, Number 3, July 2005, pp. 452–453.

4   Gülen, in an interview with Nuriye Akman, *Sabah daily*, January 23–30, 1995.

5   Gülen, in an interview with Mehmet Gündem, *Milliyet daily*, January 17, 2005; see also http://www.fethullahgulen.org/press-room/mehmet-gundems-interview/1920-gulen-qdemocracy-should-also-have-a-metaphysical-dimensionq.html.

6   Gülen, "Demokrasi Yokuşu," 02.01.2006 [Herkül online] http://www.herkul.org/kiriktesti/index.php?view=article&article_id=2846.

7   Gülen, *Windows onto the Faith: Islam and Democracy*, New Jersey: The Light, 2004, pp. 4–5.

8   The Fountain, *M. Fethullah Gülen: Essays, Perspectives, Opinions*, Rutherford, NJ: The Light, 2002, p. 19.

9   Ibid., pp. 18–19.

10 "An Interview with Fethullah Gülen," *The Muslim World*, Hartford, Vol. 95, Number 3, July 2005, p. 453.

11 Gülen, in an interview with Mehmet Gündem, *Milliyet daily*, 16 January 2005.

12 "An Interview with Fethullah Gülen," *The Muslim World*, Hartford, Vol. 95, Number 3, July 2005, p. 20.

13 Yavuz and Esposito, *Turkish Islam and the Secular State: The Gülen Movement*, NY: Syracuse University Press, 2003, p. xv.

14 Ünal and Williams (eds.), *Fethullah Gülen: Advocate of Dialogue*, New Jersey: The Fountain, 2000, p. 167.

15 Gülen, *Key Concepts in the Practice of Sufism*, p. 27.

16 The Fountain, *M. Fethullah Gülen: Essays, Perspectives, Opinions*, pp. 13–14.

17 Ibid., pp. 83–85.

18 http://hrw.org/englishwr2k8/docs/2008/01/31/usint17940.htm

19 Turkey is now the 13th most attractive country in the world for direct foreign investment.

20 Gülen, in an interview with Mehmet Gündem, *Milliyet daily*, January 16, 2005.

21 Pope Benedict XVI, "Exalted Values of Life to Counteract Secularisation," March 8, 2008.

22 Gülen, *Toward A Global Civilization of Love and Tolerance*, p. 75.

23 Mehmet Enes Ergene, *An Analysis of the Gülen Movement: Tradion Witnessing the Modern Age*, New Jersey: Tughra Books, 2008, p. 35.

CHAPTER 7: GÜLEN ON *JIHAD*, TOLERANCE, AND TERRORISM

1 Gülen, *İlayı Kelimetullah*, Istanbul: Nil Yayınları, p. 1.

2 Ibid., p. 5.

3 Gülen, *Prizma*, Vol. 2, Istanbul: Nil Yayınları, 2007, pp. 148–149.

4 Gülen, *İlayı Kelimetullah*, p. 6.

5 Gülen, *Questions and Answers about Faith*, Vol. 1, Fairfax, Virginia: The Fountain, 2000, p. 199.

6 Gülen, *İlayı Kelimetullah*, p. v.

7 Gülen, *Toward a Global Civilization of Love and Tolerance*, p. 172.

8 Karen Armstrong, "The label of Catholic terror was never used about the IRA," *The Guardian*, July, 11, 2005; http://www.guardian.co.uk/comment/story/0,,1525714,00.html/larticle_continue

9 Gülen, *Prizma*, Vol. 2, pp. 78–79.

10 Gülen, *İlayı Kelimetullah*, p. 9.

11 Gülen, *Questions & Answers about Islam*, Vol. 2, p. 159.

12 Akman, Nuriye, "Interview with M. Fethullah Gülen," *Zaman daily*, March 22–April 1, 2004.

13 Jochen Hippler, *War, Repression, Terrorism: Political Violence and Civilization in Western and Muslim Societies*, Berlin, 2006, pp. 206–207.

14 Farida Akhter, *Depopulating Bangladesh: Essays on the Politics of Fertility*, Third Edition, Dhaka: Narigrantha Prabartana, 2005, p. 67.

15 Mark Scheel, "A Communitarian Imperative: Fethullah Gülen's Model of Modern Turkey," The Fountain, Issue 61, January–February 2008.

16 http://209.85.135.132/search?q=cache:4ker1BUP5zkJ:www.fethullahgulen.org/press-room/columns/978-a-voice-of-love.pdf.

17 Ünal and Williams, *Advocate of Dialogue: Fethullah Gülen*, p. 206.

18 Taha Jabir Alalwani, *Missing Dimensions in Contemporary Islamic Movements*, Herndon, VA: The International Institute of Islamic Thought, Occasional Papers Series, No. 9, 1996.

19 "*Marifah* can be summed up as having concise knowledge about something or someone through their acts or works and attributes – knowledge which can be developed and detailed." Gülen, *Sufism*, Vol. 2, p.135.

20 Gülen, *Sufism*, Vol. 2, p.135.

21 Gülen, *Toward A Global Civilization of Love & Tolerance*, p. 150.

22 Qur'an, 5:54.

23 Qur'an, 25:63.

24 Gülen, *Sufism* Vol. 1, p. 58.

25 Gülen, *Toward a Global Civilization of Love & Tolerance*, p. 150.

26 Katherine Bullock, *Rethinking Muslim Women and the Veil: Challenging Historical & Modern Stereotypes*, Herndon, VA: The International Institute of Islamic Thought, 2003, pp. 18–20.

27 "Ideal people try to remain removed from sin, for they have designed their lives according to the Divine Law in which they believe so sincerely. And, because they always, struggle against their egos they have no time or energy to engage in ignorant pastimes or bohemian lifestyles." In Gülen, *Toward A Global Civilization of Love & Tolerance*, p. 129.

28 Davut Aydüz, quoted in Ismail Aybayrak, "The Juxtaposition of Islam and Violence," *Muslim Citizens of the Globalized World*. Robert A. Hunt, Yuksel A. Aslandogan (eds.), New Jersey: The Light, 2006, p. 127.

29 Katherine Bullock, p. 162.

30 It is also called as *Din al-Hanif,* which means the primordial religion.

31 Qur'an, 7:156–157.

32 Dilnawaz A. Siddiqui, "Middle Eastern Origins of Modern Sciences," *Muslim Contribution to World Civilization*, Herndon, VA: The International Institute of Islamic Thought, 2005, p. 60.

33 *"The Decline of the West"* (German: *Der Untergang des Abendlandes*) is a two-volume work by Oswald Spengler, the first volume of which was published in the summer of 1918. Spengler revised this volume in 1922 and published the second volume, subtitled *Perspectives of World History*, in 1923. The book includes the idea of the Muslims being Magian, Mediterranean civilizations of the antiquity such as Ancient Greece and Rome being Apollonian, and the modern Westerners being Faustian, and according to its theories we are now living in the winter time of the Faustian civilization. His description of the Faustian civilization is where the populace constantly strives for the unattainable—making the western man a proud but tragic figure, for while he strives and creates he secretly knows the actual goal will never be reached." In: http://en.wikipedia.org/wiki/The_Decline_of_the_West.

INDEX